How...

Thrive on
Stress

Thrive on
Stress

*Manage pressure
and positively thrive on it!*

JAN SUTTON
2nd edition

How To Books

Published by How To Books Ltd,
3 Newtec Place, Magdalen Road,
Oxford OX4 1RE. United Kingdom.
Tel: (01865) 793806. Fax: (01865) 248780.
email: info@howtobooks.co.uk
http://www.howtobooks.co.uk

First published 1998
Second edition 2000
Reprinted 2000

British Library Cataloguing in Publication Data.
A catalogue record for this book is available from
the British Library.

Cover design by Shireen Nathoo Design
Cover image by PhotoDisc
Cover copy by Sallyann Sheridan
Cartoons by Mike Flanagan

Produced for How To Books by Deer Park Productions
Typeset by PDQ Typesetting, Newcastle-under-Lyme, Staffs.
Printed and bound by Cromwell Press, Trowbridge, Wiltshire

NOTE: The material contained in this book is set out in good
faith for general guidance and no liability can be accepted
for loss or expense incurred as a result of relying in particular
circumstances on statements made in the book. Laws and
regulations are complex and liable to change, and readers should
check the current position with the relevant authorities before
making personal arrangements.

Contents

List of Illustrations

Is This You?

DO YOU:

Feel unable to cope? Feel anxious, panicky, tense, hopeless, worthless?
Feel constantly wound-up, irritable, angry, tired, exhausted?
Feel under constant pressure of time?

HAVE YOU:

Lost your sparkle and enthusiasm for life, your energy, your appetite, your sex drive?
Experienced a major loss – such as the loss of a loved one by death or divorce, death of an animal, child left home, lost your job or home?
Experienced a major change – got married, remarried, had an addition to the family, moved house, changed jobs?
Recently given up an addiction?

ARE YOU:

Getting recurring headaches, backache, migraines, blurred vision, dizzy turns, ringing in the ears, stomach cramps, problems with swallowing?
Experiencing negative or irrational thoughts?
Finding it difficult to concentrate or make decisions?
Having problems sleeping/waking early?
Smoking, drinking, taking more drugs than usual?
Overworking/too busy to relax?
Lacking self-confidence?
Experiencing stress at work or at home?

THIS BOOK TEACHES YOU THE SKILLS THAT WILL ENABLE YOU TO THRIVE ON STRESS:

Defining stress
Assessing your stress levels
Learning the art of relaxation
Eliminating negative mind-talk
Expressing your feelings

Communicating skilfully
Raising your self-esteem
Mastering the clock
Setting and accomplishing your
   goals

Preface
to the Second Edition

I don't do anything that's bad for me.
I don't like to be made nervous or angry.
Any time you get upset it tears down your nervous system.

(Mae West)

STRESS – A SIGN OF OUR TIMES

We live in a world full of uncertainties. However, one thing is certain: stress is here to stay and cannot be ignored.

Why is stress on the increase?

Pressures at work
The world of work is ever changing. There may be an emphasis on competition, pressure to achieve targets and meet deadlines, or to keep up with the rapid advancements in technology. The threat of redundancy may be looming large.

- Too many changes or feeling threatened can lead to stress.

Pressures to achieve
Our youth of today are under enormous pressure to achieve academically. If they succeed there is no guarantee of a job. Those who leave school without a host of qualifications may not even get a look in on the job front. Work is an important part of our lives. It provides a sense of purpose – a decent standard of living – a feeling of worth and hope for the future.

- Life without purpose or hope can lead to depression, insecurity, loss of self-esteem and confidence, boredom, frustration, feelings of failure and discontentment – all a breeding ground for stress.

Fear of violence and crime
Violence and crime are on the increase. Murder and mugging are now commonplace. Many of our homes have become fortresses to protect us from the threat of being burgled.

● Fear generates stress.

Family pressures
The fabric of family life has changed dramatically. Many families are scattered, fragmented or isolated. There are more working mothers, more single parents, more elderly people living alone, more people living on the bread line, more relationships falling apart, more pressures to keep up with the Joneses.

● Relationship breakdowns, social isolation and financial worries create the perfect conditions for stress to flourish.

Pressures on the less fortunate
There are more homeless people living in our cardboard cities, more people with mental health problems trying to survive unsupported on our streets, and more people resorting to drugs and alcohol or committing suicide to escape from today's pressures and stresses.

Stress is a unique experience
Some people are adept at coping with pressure and positively thrive on it. Others get weighed down and become ill. We are all individuals and we all react to stressful situations in our own unique way. The way we react depends on our ability to adapt to change and on our personality.

How this book can help
The aims of this book are:

● to help you gain insight into your personality

● to increase your understanding of stress and its causes

● to help you develop positive strategies that will enable you to thrive on stress.

This second edition includes additional material and inspiring quotes. The useful contacts and further reading sections have also been updated and expanded: website and email addresses have been added where applicable.

Gaining self-awareness will unlock the door to understanding. However, **to change anything requires action**. Therefore, just reading this book will not automatically bring about change – it requires a commitment to **doing the activities**. These are the steps you need to take to learn how to thrive on stress, and I recommend you work through them in the order presented.

The case studies included in this book are clinical composites and do not portray particular people. To protect confidentiality, names, events and details have been fictionalised. To avoid the clumsy formula of he/she, both pronouns are used interchangeably throughout the book.

ACKNOWLEDGEMENTS

My special thanks go to Nikki Read and Giles Lewis at How To Books for their continuing support and encouragement for my work, and to my husband Gordon for help with proofreading and for being there.

Jan Sutton

> When we cannot change a situation,
> resolution comes through the
> way we choose to handle it within ourselves.
>
> (Gerald Coffee)

1

Defining Stress

Take from our souls the strain and stress
And let our ordered lives confess
The beauty of Thy peace.

(John Greenleaf Whittier)

UNDERSTANDING WHAT STRESS MEANS

Your partner might tell you he feels stressed out. Your friend might say she feels under considerable stress. But what do they really mean?

There is a great deal of controversy about the term 'stress', and because it is such a highly complex phenomenon, the task of defining it is difficult. To appreciate its complexity, let us look at four situations and see how two different people might react.

Situation 1
Two people are asked to give a public speech.
Person A.   Views it as a challenge and feels elated.
               Behaviour → Gives a glowing performance.
Person B.   Sees it as threatening and is filled with anxiety.
               Behaviour → Makes an excuse not to do it.

Situation 2
Two people whose jobs have been made redundant.
Person A.   Views it as an opportunity to learn new skills and feels motivated.
               Behaviour → Prepares a CV, and joins a job club.
Person B.   Sees it as threatening and is filled with fear.
               Behaviour → Sits at home and procrastinates.

Situation 3
Two people are invited to attend a job interview.

Person A.   Views it as a challenge and feels confident.
               Behaviour → Researches into the company and
               performs well.
Person B.   Sees it as threatening and is filled with apprehension.
               Behaviour → Decides not to attend.

Situation 4
Two people preparing for Christmas.
Person A.   Views it as a chance to enjoy life and feels excited.
               Behaviour → Puts decorations up and arranges a
               party.
Person B.   Sees it as threatening and is filled with frustration.
               Behaviour → Has a row with her partner.

From these four brief examples we can see that what stimulates and
excites one person may be stressful and provoke anxiety in another.
This is what makes the task of defining stress so difficult, because it
means different things to different individuals. However, if we look
again at the four examples, we can see that there are similarities. In
all four examples, person B perceives the situation as threatening.
Therefore one definition of stress could be:

**Stress is a response to a situation which a person
perceives as threatening**

RECOGNISING THAT THERE IS A POSITIVE SIDE TO STRESS

We all experience stress. Indeed, a healthy amount of stress is a
powerful motivating force, which we can positively thrive on.
However, if stress levels become too high, all positive stimulation is
replaced by exhaustion, and we begin to find it difficult to cope. An
overload of stress over a lengthy period can lead to burnout or
eventual breakdown.

Identifying the three levels of stress
Under-stimulation as well as over-stimulation can both be sources of
potential stress. Take, for example, a young woman at home all day
with young children. When her husband gets in from work she tells
him she has had a stressful day. He might assume that her stress is

caused by the demands of the children, whereas it could be caused by her not having any adult company, or because she has no satisfying work to stimulate her. Under-stimulation and over-stimulation can drain our energy reserves, whereas optimum stimulation mobilises our energy.

The three levels of stress, therefore, are:

1. too little stress (under-stimulation)

2. peak performance stress (optimum stimulation)

3. too much stress (over-stimulation).

CASE STUDY 1 – BURNT-OUT BERNICE

Bernice set up her own aromatherapy practice. She loved helping people and enjoyed talking to her clients. Initially she was full of enthusiasm, had boundless energy and put her all into her work. Her hard work paid dividends; within a year she had built a very successful business.

However, after about three years she noticed that she was feeling very tired and her enthusiasm was waning. As her energy levels decreased so did her ability to sleep. Everyday tasks became more difficult to cope with, and she started feeling an element of resentment towards her clients for making so many demands on her energy and time. She began to get headaches and backache, and on waking each morning felt as if she'd hardly slept a wink. Normally a calm and relaxed person, she was surprised at what a short fuse she was on. She would suddenly explode at her husband for no reason, and was rather cool towards her clients.

She pushed herself harder and harder to try and cope with her increasing workload, despite a large part of her wanting to run away and say 'to hell with everything'. After pushing herself in this way for a further six months, Bernice collapsed. She was admitted to hospital suffering from burnout. Bernice had become starved of vital fuel. She had nothing left in reserve to keep her going, rather like a car that's run out of petrol and hasn't been properly maintained.

If you can see yourself following the same path as Bernice, it is imperative that you take action now before you reach crisis point and collapse like she did.

CASE STUDY 2 – OPTIMUM OWEN

Owen was stimulated by his work. Very little ruffled him, and he thrived under pressure. He was full of enthusiasm, confidence and energy. He took care of his health and ensured he got adequate rest. Owen had the ability to stay on top of things and performed well in everything he did. He was very much in control of his life, unlike burnt-out Bernice, who lost control when the pressure became too great.

IDENTIFYING THE EFFECTS OF STRESS ON THE BODY

When we perceive a situation to be threatening, we have a built-in alarm system that prepares us for action – to deal with the threat or to run away from it. This is commonly referred to as the **fight or flight** response. Figure 1 shows the effects of stress on the body.

Understanding the fight or flight response

To demonstrate the fight or flight response more clearly, let us look again at the four situations mentioned earlier.

In situation 1   person B talks himself out of giving a public speech (*takes flight*).

In situation 2   person B sits at home and does nothing (*takes flight*).

In situation 3   person B talks himself out of attending the interview (*takes flight*).

In situation 4   person B has a row with her partner (*fights*).

In situations 1, 2 and 3, person B has taken flight. However, their response is inappropriate because they have avoided confronting the source of their stress. In situation 4, person B has adopted the fight response. This response is also inappropriate because she has fought with words, rather than dealing directly with the source of her stress – what lies behind her frustration. If the source of stress is not faced up to and dealt with effectively, energy released at the 'threatening stage' can get bottled up instead of being used up, which over time can result in a wide variety of distressing symptoms.

• People who experience high levels of stress live in a constant state of readiness to fight or take flight. They are always on **RED ALERT**.

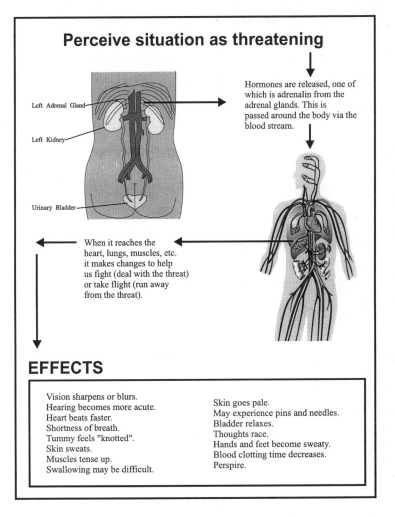

Perceive situation as threatening

Left Adrenal Gland

Left Kidney

Urinary Bladder

Hormones are released, one of which is adrenalin from the adrenal glands. This is passed around the body via the blood stream.

When it reaches the heart, lungs, muscles, etc. it makes changes to help us fight (deal with the threat) or take flight (run away from the threat).

EFFECTS

Vision sharpens or blurs.
Hearing becomes more acute.
Heart beats faster.
Shortness of breath.
Tummy feels "knotted".
Skin sweats.
Muscles tense up.
Swallowing may be difficult.

Skin goes pale.
May experience pins and needles.
Bladder relaxes.
Thoughts race.
Hands and feet become sweaty.
Blood clotting time decreases.
Perspire.

Fig. 1. The effects of stress on the body.

Summary

If we perceive a situation as threatening, our body prepares us to take action (fight or take flight). If we respond to the threat inappropriately (*eg* by avoiding it, or making excuses), energy released at the action stage remains in our body, which can lead to a range of stressful symptoms.

He that fights and runs away, may live to fight another day.

(Anonymous)

STUDYING THE FOUR COMPONENTS OF STRESS

Stress has four parts:
1. mental symptoms
2. physical symptoms
3. emotional symptoms
4. behavioural symptoms.

Mental symptoms

Some of the mental symptoms associated with stress include:

lapses in memory
persistent negative thoughts
putting tasks off
less sensitive than normal

loss of concentration
inability to make decisions
inability to get tasks completed

Physical symptoms

Some of the physical symptoms associated with stress include:

heart palpitations
backache
ringing in the ears
stomach disorders
constipation or diarrhoea
cold hands and feet
passing urine frequently
indigestion
sore throats in the evening
vague aches and pains
difficulty getting to sleep
exhaustion

frequent headaches
jaw ache
pains in the back of the neck
leg and feet cramps
irritable bowel
scalp tight and tingly
sore and tired eyes
skin problems
tiredness
excessive sweating
waking early

Emotional symptoms

Some of the emotional symptoms associated with stress include:

bursting into tears easily
loss of humour
reduced self-esteem
loss of enthusiasm
cynicism
more nervous than usual
irritable or more angry than
    normal

depression
loss of self-confidence
poor self-image
mood swings
anxiety
feeling vulnerable

Behavioural symptoms
Some of the behavioural symptoms associated with stress include:

more accident prone than usual
poor work performance
self-neglect
loss of sex drive
loss of appetite or overeating
   for comfort
speech impairments
overworking
withdrawal from supportive
   relationships

compulsions/obsessions
aggressive
too busy to relax
increased drinking, smoking,
   drug-taking
poor time management
hyperactivity
unsociability
eating disorders
self-harm

These lists are by no means exhaustive. As already mentioned, we are all unique individuals who will respond to pressure or stress in our own unique ways.

High levels of stress can lead to anxiety

Possible physical symptoms of anxiety

palpitations
panic attacks
pain in the heart region
nervous dyspepsia
nervous headaches
   and migraines

nervous rashes
constipation
digestive disorders
tension in the mind,
   the brain, the
   whole self

shaking
sweating
butterflies in
   the stomach
nervous diarrhoea

Possible feelings associated with anxiety

afraid
concerned
distressed
fatigued
nervous
panicky
tense
unsettled

agitated
depressed
disturbed
fretful
overwrought
restless
troubled
worried

apprehensive
disquieted
edgy
irritable
pained
stressed
uneasy
weary

Possible effects associated with anxiety
- Difficulties with interpersonal relationships.

- Person may try to keep up a facade – pretending all is well.

- Sensitive to noise.

- Sexual difficulties.

- Person gets upset very easily.

- Person over-reacts to situations – particularly to criticism.

- Inability to relax.

- Difficulties sleeping – can't get comfortable or toss and turn.

- Speech impairments – person may talk very rapidly or their flow of words is interrupted.

- Phobias such as agoraphobia or claustrophobia may develop.

- Obsessions such as constant checking, handwashing, cleaning or repeated counting may develop.

- Person loses their ability to think clearly and their ability to concentrate.

- Hands may become shaky – writing becomes jerky – letters may be missed out of words.

UNDERSTANDING PANIC ATTACKS

A panic attack can occur if a person becomes overwhelmed by anxiety. Panic attacks are terrifying for the sufferer. The person may believe they are having a heart attack, feel faint or experience dizzy turns. During a panic attack the heart pounds, palms may sweat, there may be ringing in the ears. Vision can become blurred and spots may appear before the eyes, like little tadpoles floating by. Panic can aptly be described as an **irrational and magnified form of fear**.

Note:

If you have been experiencing any of the symptoms described in this chapter and they are persisting, you would be well advised to seek professional help from your GP or a Stress Management Counsellor.

IDENTIFYING CAUSES OF STRESS

The causes of stress are many and varied. In the 1960s, Thomas Holmes and Richard Rahe, two American psychologists, developed a scale of 43 life events considered to be stressful (the Holmes-Rahe

Social Adjustment Scale). These were then ranked in order of the degree of stress associated with each event. Listed below are the top ten life events identified through their research, together with the scores assigned to each event.

Life event	Score
Death of a spouse (partner)	100
Divorce	73
Marital separation	65
Jail term	63
Death of a close family member	63
Personal injury or illness	53
Marriage	50
Dismissal from work	47
Marital reconciliation	45
Retirement	45

From this list we can see that it's not only traumatic life events that can prove stressful. Even welcome ones, such as getting married, can generate stress. From research carried out with groups of students who attend my stress awareness and management courses, I have discovered that there are other life events and situations considered to be high on the stress list. These include:

- loss of a parent by divorce or separation
- being a working mum and running a home
- being a single parent, working, running a home and trying to make ends meet
- relationship conflicts
- being a step-parent/step-daughter/step-son
- extended families
- financially supporting two families
- loss of a job
- unemployment
- job insecurity

- giving up hope of ever getting a job
- being self-employed
- financial worries or mounting debts
- coping with a disability
- giving up an addiction – drinking, drugs, cigarettes, gambling, food
- longer holidays – too much time together with partner, children, in-laws
- falling out with the neighbours, family members or friends.

It's important to bear in mind, though, that every individual is different, and what might become a potential source of stress to one person might be a source of stimulation to another. It very much depends on a person's personality and their ability to adjust to change. Too many changes over a short period of time increase the likelihood of stress.

EXAMINING CAUSE AND EFFECT

Case study 3 – Anxious Anna
It was the beginning of a busy day for Anna, as she was about to start facilitating a new counselling course. She got up early to allow herself plenty of time to prepare her materials. Shortly before she was scheduled to leave, her friend arrived, distressed and needing a shoulder to cry on. When Anna was ready to depart, she could not find her flipchart pad with the diagrams she had prepared for the course. This threw Anna into a panic and her heart started pounding. By the time she found it, she was running very late, so she drove like fury to the venue, arriving five minutes before the course was due to start. She felt flustered and anxious. Consequently, Anna's performance was below par.

Analysis of Anna's situation
1. Anna's friend turning up put her behind schedule (*cause*).
2. She could not find her flipchart pad, which put her schedule even further behind (*cause*).
3. Her heart started pounding (*physical symptom – effect*).

4. She felt panicky, flustered and anxious (*emotional symptoms – effect*).

5. She drove like fury (*behavioural symptom – effect*).

6. Her performance was below par (*outcome*).

However, to get to the root cause of Anna's stress, we need to look at what was happening to her thoughts – what she was saying to herself (mind-talk). It went something like this:

- 'Why did my friend have to turn up now? It's going to make me late.'
- 'I can't leave her when she's so upset.'
- 'Why didn't I look for my flipchart pad last night?'
- 'I'm definitely going to be late and that will be disastrous.'

So, as you can see, it all started in Anna's mind. It was what she was saying to herself (mind-talk) that brought on physical symptoms, which sparked stressful feelings, which led to negative behaviour and a negative outcome. Figure 2 demonstrates how negative mind-talk triggers off a negative stress cycle.

BREAKING OUT OF THE NEGATIVE STRESS CYCLE

To begin to break free from the negative stress cycle we need to:

1. gain awareness into our personal stress triggers

2. learn the art of relaxation

3. monitor our mind-talk – what we are saying to ourselves

4. challenge negative mind-talk.

WRITING A PERSONAL DEVELOPMENT JOURNAL

Let diaries, therefore, be brought into use.

(Francis Bacon)

Writing a personal development journal can be an invaluable tool for measuring progress. It can help you see clearly where you have come from and identify areas you need to work on. It is also useful for recording your goals for the future – where you would like to be.

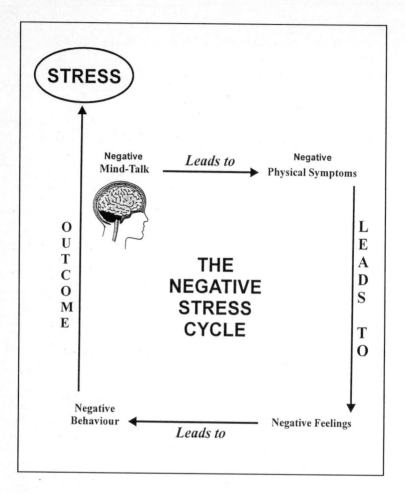

Fig. 2. The negative stress cycle.

At the end of each chapter in this book you will find suggestions of what to include in your journal. However, these suggestions are only intended as a guide: the most important thing is to record whatever will help you personally.

Keeping a personal journal may seem a chore or self-indulgent at first. However, do try to persevere. It is a wonderful way of getting to know yourself better, and increased self-awareness will help you understand other people better too. Writing your thoughts and feelings out on paper can be very therapeutic and revealing, so look on it as a precious gift you can give yourself.

What is a diary as a rule? A document useful to the person who keeps it, dull to the contemporary who reads it, invaluable to the student, centuries afterwards, who treasures it!

(Dame Ellen Terry)

KEEPING YOUR PERSONAL DEVELOPMENT JOURNAL

Most of the time we think we're sick, it's all in the mind.

(Thomas Wolfe)

1. Record the three levels of stress.

2. Record the four components of stress.

3. Record any major life events you have experienced over the past year.

4. Record what you need to do to get out of the negative stress cycle.

5. Write a brief definition of what stress means to you personally.

6. Make a note of symptoms associated with panic attacks.

2

Assessing Your Stress Levels

To become the spectator of one's life is to escape the suffering of life.

(Oscar Wilde)

IDENTIFYING SYMPTOMS AND CAUSES

The aim of this chapter is to help you get a clearer self-picture of your personal stressors and their causes. There are activities to help you pinpoint symptoms of stress, to establish whether you are in the right job, and to identify whether your personality type makes you susceptible, or resilient, to stress. There are no right or wrong answers. The important thing is to be honest with yourself.

Carrying out the activities

To gain maximum benefit from the activities, **take your time**. Remember, Rome wasn't built in a day. If you rush through them, you might miss a precious gem of insight that can help you to help yourself. As you work through the activities focus your mind on the following questions:

1. Are there any situations in my life at the moment that are causing me stress?

2. Are there any people in my life at the moment that are contributing to my stress?

3. Is there anything I can do *right now* to reduce my stress?

Developing your self-picture

Genius is one per cent inspiration and ninety-nine per cent perspiration.

(Thomas Alva Edison)

Imagine yourself as a photographer wanting to produce a winning picture. How would you achieve this?

- *Perspiration.* You would start as an amateur producing distorted pictures. You might get things out of focus, too close, too far away, to one side, or cut bits out of the picture.

- *Dedication.* You practise, and gradually your pictures start improving. You begin to produce more accurate pictures. You start to get things more into focus.

- *Inspiration.* You gain confidence, and start coming up with creative ideas that give your pictures that extra something. You get your pictures fully in focus. You like what you have produced and can see clearly that your picture is a winner, and nobody did it for you. You produced your winning picture through your own hard work and determination.

Record any revealing insights in your personal development journal as you go along, bearing in mind that **awareness is the key that unlocks the door to understanding – to developing a clearer self-picture.**

A moment's insight is sometimes worth a life's experience.
(Oliver Wendell Holmes)

ACTIVITY 1 – Pinpointing symptoms of stress

Mental symptoms – tick the appropriate box   Yes No

	Yes	No
I used to be good at making decisions but am now finding it more difficult.	☑	☐
I find it difficult to concentrate.	☑	☐
I have started worrying about everything.	☑	☐
I find it difficult to think straight.	☑	☐
I keep forgetting things.	☑	☐
I am making more mistakes than usual.	☑	☐
I am less sensitive than usual.	☐	☑
I keep getting negative or irrational thoughts.	☑	☐

Physical symptoms – tick the appropriate box   Yes No

I get heart palpitations.   ☐ ☐

I get dizzy turns.   ☐ ☐

I get frequent headaches.   ☐ ☐

I get jaw ache.   ☐ ☐

I get pains in the back of my neck.   ☐ ☐

I get tension across my shoulders.   ☐ ☐

My stomach often feels 'knotted'.   ☐ ☐

I get leg and feet cramps.   ☐ ☐

I get frequent bouts of indigestion.   ☐ ☐

I get ringing in my ears.   ☐ ☐

I get diarrhoea.   ☐ ☐

I get a sore throat in the evening.   ☐ ☐

My breathing is shallow.   ☐ ☐

My hands and feet often feel cold.   ☐ ☐

My mouth gets dry.   ☐ ☐

My eyes get tired and sore.   ☐ ☐

I perspire a lot.   ☐ ☐

I want to pass urine frequently.   ☐ ☐

I am losing weight rapidly without dieting.   ☐ ☐

My weight is spiralling.   ☐ ☐

I feel tired most of the time.   ☐ ☐

I pick up every virus that's going round.   ☐ ☐

I am susceptible to allergies.   ☐ ☐

I get unexplained skin rashes or irritation.   ☐ ☐

Emotional symptoms – tick the appropriate box   Yes No

I keep bursting into tears.   ☐ ☐

I have lost my self-confidence.   ☐ ☐

I get mood swings. ☐ ☐

I feel vulnerable. ☐ ☐

I feel drained. ☐ ☐

My self-esteem is low. ☐ ☐

I have a poor self-image. ☐ ☐

I am more irritable than usual. ☐ ☐

I keep getting angry. ☐ ☐

I feel apprehensive. ☐ ☐

I am more cynical than usual. ☐ ☐

I feel worthless. ☐ ☐

I feel tense. ☐ ☐

I feel unhappy. ☐ ☐

I feel as if something terrible is going to happen. ☐ ☐

I feel as if I am falling apart at the seams. ☐ ☐

I feel frightened. ☐ ☐

I feel helpless. ☐ ☐

I feel hopeless. ☐ ☐

I feel depressed. ☐ ☐

I get upset if I am criticised. ☐ ☐

I feel nervous. ☐ ☐

I feel anxious. ☐ ☐

I have lost my sparkle and enthusiasm. ☐ ☐

Behavioural symptoms – tick the appropriate box Yes No

I find it impossible to relax. ☐ ☐

I am more accident prone than usual. ☐ ☐

I can't switch off when I go to bed (my thoughts
   won't stop racing). ☐ ☐

I wake early in the morning. ☐ ☐

I wake feeling tired. ☐ ☐

My alcohol consumption has increased. ☐ ☐

I am taking non-prescribed drugs without
   consulting my GP. ☐ ☐

I am smoking more than usual. ☐ ☐

My time management is poor. ☐ ☐

I have lost interest in sex. ☐ ☐

I neglect myself. ☐ ☐

I bring work home with me. ☐ ☐

I rarely see my friends any more. ☐ ☐

I have become obsessive. ☐ ☐

I talk non-stop. ☐ ☐

I lose the thread of what I am saying. ☐ ☐

I have no time for leisure activities. ☐ ☐

I am too busy to relax. ☐ ☐

FOCUSING ON YOUR SELF-PICTURE

1. Make a note of any Yes boxes you have ticked.

2. How many Yes boxes have you ticked in each section?

3. How long have you been experiencing these symptoms?

4. Are they getting worse?

5. Which symptoms are concerning you the most?

6. Use your imagination to create inspiration:

What could you do to alleviate these symptoms?

Your personal development journal
In your personal journal record the following:

1. A complete list of the symptoms you are currently experiencing,

paying particular attention to whether these symptoms are more from one particular group; for example, are they mainly emotional symptoms?

2. Any strategies you have come up with to start alleviating the symptoms.

EXPLORING CAUSES OF STRESS AT WORK

Stress at work is becoming a major problem that cannot be ignored. It is estimated that 'every day in the UK, some 270,000 people take time off work for stress-related illness' (Rowena Rees, *The Sunday Times*, Stress Manager, Part 1: In The Workplace, 18 May 1997). The effects of stress are therefore very costly both in human terms for individuals and in resource terms for employers.

Concerns about the stigma of stress

Although there is a growing awareness and acceptance of stress, many people are still reluctant to admit they are suffering from its effects. They worry about the word 'stress' appearing on their sick note or being recorded in their medical records, viewing it as some sort of weakness or defect of character, or carrying negative overtones that will jeopardise their career prospects. Employers are starting to realise that stress is a sign of the times we live in, and some companies now provide stress counselling for their employees. However, from clients who come to me for stress counselling, it is evident that some choose not to take up free counselling offered by their employers, preferring to pay privately for treatment rather than risk their employers or colleagues finding out.

Why is stress at work on the increase?

Groups of teachers who attend my stress awareness and management workshops have provided valuable insight into why stress is on the increase at work. Here are some of the reasons identified:

- Travelling to work – the volume of traffic, getting stuck in traffic jams.
- Unrealistic deadlines.
- Being expected to work miracles.
- Lack of job security.

- Poor working conditions (noise, space, equipment).
- Poor internal communications.
- Not feeling valued or appreciated.
- Poor forward planning.
- Too much work.
- Constant interruptions.
- Managers who come with ten commandments rather than four-and-a-half tentative suggestions or proposals.
- A culture of blame – not one of problem-solving.
- The volume of paperwork – especially if repetitive and unnecessary.
- Lack of leadership and support.
- Inequity of job division and reward.
- External directives impacting on internal priorities.
- Lack of opportunity for career progression.
- Mistakes.
- Frequent procedural changes.
- Lack of unstructured time during the day.
- Being expected to have certain skills or knowledge without being given training.
- Too many meetings outside working hours – impinging on private life.
- Expected to be all things to all people.
- Responsible for people and things.
- The changing role of the teacher.
- Expected to be social workers without the skills or adequate backup.
- Inability to prioritise.
- Feeling responsible for students' success/failure.
- Open door policy.
- New courses...new courses...new courses!

Analysing the stress risk factor at work

From research carried out into the most stressful professions, teaching comes high on the list, along with the police force, prison service, fire brigade, ambulance service, social work, armed forces and nursing. Occupations involving an element of danger, risk or the unknown, or where people are **directly responsible for other people**, could come under the classification of **high stress risk** jobs, whereas people in jobs where they are **responsible to people** or **responsible for machines or a service** could come under the classification of **lower stress risk** jobs. Would you agree?

Think about your own job. Would you consider it to be a high or low stress risk job? People in high stress risk jobs often thrive on the challenge of being faced with the unknown. They seem to need a surge of adrenalin to stimulate them into giving of their best. They also need the ability to remain calm in a crisis.

The exception to the rule

Every person is a unique individual and no matter what job we do we can still be vulnerable to stress. At the end of the day it comes down to several factors:

1. how we cope with change

2. the type of person we are

3. whether there are other things going on in our lives outside work that are creating stress.

In his book *How to Counsel People at Work* (How To Books), John Humphries supports point 3 by saying:

> Most of the causes of stress are domestic in origin; they are then exacerbated by pressures at work. These extra pressures are in turn taken home where they are added to the existing problems. This results in a vicious circle of ever increasing stress which – if not diagnosed and treated – can in extreme cases lead to mental breakdown and even suicide.

One final important point to remember here is that as soon as we start feeling under pressure our energy reserves become depleted and we are at risk of moving into the stress domain.

GETTING A CLEARER SELF-PICTURE

ACTIVITY 2 – Establishing whether you are in the right job

Tick Y for yes or N for no.   Y   N

Did you always plan to do the kind of work
   you are now doing? ☐ ☐

Has your career proved as satisfying as you
   hoped it would be? ☐ ☐

Would you choose the same career if you had
   the choice over again? ☐ ☐

Would you encourage your child to take up
   your kind of work? ☐ ☐

Does your job make the fullest use of your
   potential? ☐ ☐

Are your educational/professional qualifications
   relevant in your job? ☐ ☐

Do you have the opportunity to increase
   your knowledge and skills? ☐ ☐

Is there a balance between enough variety
   and too much? ☐ ☐

Do you look forward to going to work? ☐ ☐

Do you often take work home in the evenings
   or at the weekends? ☐ ☐

Do you enjoy talking about your job outside
   working hours? ☐ ☐

Are you happy to be back at work following a holiday? ☐ ☐

If you left your present job, would you look
   for another like it? ☐ ☐

Do you get along with your immediate boss? ☐ ☐

Do you get along with the majority of your colleagues? ☐ ☐

Would you be comfortable socialising with
   your colleagues away from work? ☐ ☐

Are you clear about what is expected of you in your job? ☐ ☐

Do you feel you have a balance between enough
   responsibility and too much? ☐ ☐

Are you satisfied with your promotional prospects? ☐ ☐

Are you satisfied with the level of your salary? ☐ ☐

If there are fringe benefits, are they satisfactory? ☐ ☐

Is your job reasonably secure? ☐ ☐

Are your special abilities appreciated by the organisation? ☐ ☐

Is the climate in the organisation conducive to
   getting the best out of you? ☐ ☐

Do you consider your organisation cares for
its employees? □ □
Would you recommend your organisation to a friend
who was job hunting? □ □
Are you actively seeking another job? □ □

Interpreting your scores
Add your scores:

● If your **Y score** is between **19 and 27** you do not have a problem.
You are generally contented in your job.

● If your **Y score** is between **10 and 18** there is a degree of
uncertainty about your work. Look at your N scores, and
consider whether there is anything you can do about changing
the Ns to Ys.

● If your **Y score** is between **0 and 9** there is definite incompatibility
between yourself and your job. Consider carefully your N scores
and see if there is anything you can do about changing them to Ys.

The fact that you are still in the same job does not necessarily mean
that you find satisfaction in it. Neither does it mean that you have
chosen the right career. Every year hundreds of bored or frustrated
people drop out of their jobs and take up a completely different type
of work. Some arrive there by way of a hobby. Many more like their
jobs well enough, but change employers, seeking more financial
reward, status or opportunities for advancement.
(Printed with kind permission of William Stewart, *Stress Workbook*,
October 1991.)

UNDERSTANDING PERSONALITY TYPES AND STRESS

Research carried out by doctors and psychologists has identified a
personality type considered to be particularly at risk of stress. The
term used to describe this personality type is **the 'A' type personality**.

CASE STUDY 4 – 'A' TYPE ALAN

Alan was born to be a high achiever. It was expected of him. Both
his parents were ambitious and highly successful in their chosen

careers. Alan believed he was loved conditionally by his parents, not for who he was, but for what he achieved.

At the age of seven Alan was packed off to boarding school. He took this as a sign that his parents didn't love him. He felt rejected, very alone and abandoned. Alan tried desperately to win the love and approval of his parents by working hard at school. When he went home during the holidays, not once did his parents ever ask whether he was happy at school. All they seemed interested in was what grades he had achieved in his exams. Anything less than top marks was greeted with disdain: 'Surely you could have done better than that' or 'You really must try harder if you want to succeed like your father'.

Alan strives for perfection

Alan did try harder – at everything. He became achievement motivated (an 'A' type characteristic), aiming to get top marks in every subject. On the sports field he was highly competitive (an 'A' type characteristic). He was never content being just a team player – he had to make captain, otherwise he lost interest. Even in a chess game, the one leisure pursuit he allowed himself, he had to win. He believed that if he came top in everything his parents might start to love him. By the time he was 16 Alan carried the firm beliefs: 'I must succeed at all costs, I must win, I must strive for perfection'. Sadly, however, no matter how well he did, the loving words he yearned for from his parents were never forthcoming.

Alan's parents decide his future

Alan didn't know what career to pursue, and didn't have to give it much thought. His parents had already decided for him – naturally he would follow in his father's footsteps and become a lawyer. He felt he had no right to question his parents' decision – *after all, parents know best*. At university and college he continued to work hard, resisting any temptation to relax and have fun. His work and study came before everything (an 'A' type characteristic). He achieved a first class honours degree in law.

Alan follows in his father's footsteps

Because of his father's excellent reputation and connections, Alan was soon snapped up by a highly respected firm of London solicitors. His parents were proud of what he had achieved, regularly boasting about his accomplishments to their friends and colleagues. But never once did Alan hear his parents tell him, or anyone else, *what a wonderful son he was*. This further reinforced Alan's belief that the only way to gain any recognition was through achieving.

Alan climbs to the top

Alan was deeply committed to his work (an 'A' type characteristic), and very quickly climbed to the top of his profession. Work poured in and he prided himself on never losing a case. He was continually attending to several jobs at once (an 'A' type characteristic), and there were never enough hours in the day to complete the tasks he set himself. Often he would take work home and burn the midnight oil paying meticulous attention to the details of his clients' cases. He drove himself and others hard, was inflexible and impatient, and intolerant of his own and other people's weaknesses (all 'A' type characteristics). He also found it impossible to relax (an 'A' type characteristic).

Alan becomes disillusioned

When Alan was 38 he starting getting disillusioned with life, but couldn't understand why. He thought to himself: 'OK, so my parents don't show me any love, but I've been very fortunate in other areas of my life. I've come from a privileged background, had a first class education, and I've got material possessions that would be the envy of many a man. What right have I got to be disillusioned?' However, despite telling himself these things, he still felt as if there was a big empty space in his life. Even the fruits of his success, a magnificent house overlooking the river Thames and a brand new Porsche in the drive, did nothing to fill the emptiness he felt inside.

Alan starts experiencing stress symptoms

To add to his misery, Alan started getting distressing symptoms – chronic indigestion, stomach pains and blurred vision. He found it difficult to concentrate on his work, and instead of his usual hyper-alertness (an 'A' type characteristic), started forgetting things and making mistakes. For the first time in his career he lost a major case which resulted in his client being sentenced to life imprisonment.

Alan takes things personally

Alan felt he had failed his client, failed himself and failed his parents. This was just too much for him to bear. He went home, swigged down a few stiff gins, took a bottle of pain killers, got into bed and prayed for a quick end to his misery. As luck would have it his parents called by. They became very concerned when they couldn't get a reply to their knock – feeling certain Alan must be in because his car was parked in the drive. They telephoned the police, who came and forced the door. Alan was rushed to casualty, where his stomach was pumped out. From there, at the request of his parents, he was transferred for assessment to a private psychiatric hospital. Alan was diagnosed as suffering from chronic stress and depression.

Alan experiences unconditional acceptance

One evening a warm and friendly nurse sat at his bedside and asked: 'Alan, what has been happening in your life that made you want to end it all?' Alan felt the tears well up in his eyes, which he frantically tried to swallow (he'd been taught that big boys don't cry). The lump in his throat nearly choked him as he struggled to stifle his tears. The nurse sat silently waiting for him to answer. Her question had hit on a very raw nerve, and when he opened his mouth the tears soon followed. The nurse sat listening to him for an hour and a half as he poured out his anguish. She didn't criticise or judge him. All she said was: 'It sounds as if you have been having a very difficult time. Would you like me to come back and see you again tomorrow?' Alan replied: 'Yes please, I'd really appreciate that'. After the nurse had gone he felt as if a very heavy burden had been lifted off his shoulders. What meant more to him than anything was that she had given him her time, she had listened to him and she had accepted him unconditionally.

Alan takes stock

With continued support from the nurse, the doctors and the patients in the daily therapy groups, Alan started taking stock of his life. It was very painful for him to recognise that he had spent his entire life striving to be perfect in an effort to be loved and approved of by his parents. He scrutinised his career, seeing quite clearly that he hadn't really wanted to be a lawyer, but felt he'd had no choice in the matter. When one patient asked him: 'What would you really like to do?' he couldn't answer, but it started him thinking.

Alan falls in love

Alan made a decision. Feeling a bit like a rebellious teenager – albeit a bit late – he resigned from his job, which met with his parents' disapproval. This left him feeling sad, but his need to please them wasn't so urgent any more. He had more pressing things to attend to. He had fallen head over heels in love with the warm and empathic nurse, and couldn't believe his luck when she accepted his proposal of marriage.

Alan changes direction

Alan and his new wife went on a cruise for their honeymoon. While they were away relaxing and having fun, Alan had time to think and the seeds of a new future were planted. He decided he would like to help deprived youngsters. Deprivation was something he could closely identify with, despite his privileged background. When the cruise was over Alan did several things:

1. He purchased a boat and took sailing lessons. When he was a competent sailor he offered free holidays to underprivileged children.

2. He trained as a teacher and became a lecturer in law.

3. He confronted his parents with how he felt about the way they had treated him as a child. This was excruciatingly painful, especially when they both said: 'After all we've done for you, how can you be so ungrateful?' However, over time they started to think about what Alan had said, and he couldn't believe his ears, when, one day, calling on him unexpectedly, his Mum greeted him with a hug and said: 'I do love you dearly'. His Dad also put his arms round him saying: 'I love you too, son'. After a very emotional and tearful scene, his Mum added the words: 'I'm sorry, we never told you before. It's not easy to say "I love you" if you've never heard the words from your own parents. I guess mine loved me too, but perhaps they didn't know how to say the words either.'

Alan feels loved unconditionally

Needless to say, Alan was ecstatic. Although the big empty space in his life had been almost filled to the brim with love from his adoring wife, hearing those three precious words from his parents left him feeling as if his cup was flowing over.

This lengthy case study has been included here for a specific purpose. It not only highlights the characteristics of the 'A' type personality, it also draws attention to some other very important topics which we will be addressing later in the book:

1. The effects of negative mind-talk, and rigid beliefs.

2. How self-esteem is influenced by our early childhood experiences.

3. How relationships can be improved by expressing our feelings openly and honestly.

4. How good communication can prevent misunderstandings arising.

We will be revisiting Alan in Chapter 4.

BRINGING YOUR SELF-PICTURE MORE FULLY INTO FOCUS

ACTIVITY 3 – Establishing whether you possess 'A' type personality characteristics

Tick the response which most fits your personality.

Do you:	Yes	No
Get uptight if you don't finish whatever you have started?	☑	☐
Hate being late for appointments?	☑	☐
Consider yourself to be highly competitive?	☐	☑
Finish other people's sentences or interrupt them?	☑	☐
Always go full speed ahead at everything?	☐	☑
Get frustrated if you are kept waiting?	☑	☐
Sometimes rush a task so you can get on with the next one?	☑	☐
Attempt to do more than one task at a time?	☐	☑
Put your point across forcefully?	☐	☑
Want approval for a job well done (especially from your superiors)?	☑	☐
Always feel overly responsible?	☐	☑
Drive yourself and others hard?	☑	☐
Hold your feelings in check?	☑	☐
Consider yourself to be very ambitious and want quick promotion?	☐	☑
Set yourself rigid deadlines?	☐	☑
Harbour aggressive feelings?	☑	☐
Put your work before everything else in your life?	☐	☑
Take your work very seriously?	☐	☑
Pay meticulous attention to detail?	☐	☑
Strive for perfection?	☐	☑
Feel guilty relaxing if there are jobs left undone?	☑	☐
See yourself as a racehorse rather than a tortoise?	☐	☑
Feel tense most of the time?	☐	☑

Find it difficult to delegate believing no one else
can do a job as well as you can?

Find it difficult to laugh at yourself?

Prefer to be *doing* rather than just *being*?

Get so wrapped up in your work that you fail to
notice what other people are doing or saying?

Believe that winning is more important than
participating?

Interpreting your scores
Check your **Yes** scores.

- **Yes** scores point to 'A' type characteristics. Therefore, the higher
  your number of Yes scores the more you may be putting yourself
  at risk of stress-related illness. If you have answered Yes to all
  the questions this indicates a very high level of 'A' type
  characteristics and you need to take immediate action to avoid
  the risk of over-stimulation or burnout. Look carefully at your
  Yes scores and consider what you can do to work towards
  optimum stimulation.

Check your **No** scores.

- **No** scores point to an easy going personality. If your No scores
  are high you are unlikely to be at risk of stress. However, a high
  No score could possibly indicate under-stimulation, or procrastination, so beware. Look carefully at your No scores and
  consider whether there is any action you need to take to work
  towards optimum stimulation. We will be looking more at the
  effects of procrastination in Chapter 8 (Mastering the Clock).

SUMMARY OF 'A' TYPE CHARACTERISTICS
'A' types are:

- achievement motivated – they have a strong desire to be approved
  of

- highly competitive – in almost all areas of their lives

- restless – they have extreme difficulty relaxing

- hyper-alert

- always racing against the clock and doing several tasks at once

- overly responsible

- intolerant of their own weaknesses and other people's – they drive themselves and others hard

- deeply committed to their work – other areas of their lives are often neglected

- aggressive (which they sometimes repress), impatient, and inflexible.

William Stewart in his *Stress Workbook* (1991) says:

> Much of the work ethos of the 1990s is geared toward the 'A' type personality, for whom competition and excessive hours present a constant challenge. Many young people already have their behaviour shaped into the type 'A' pattern as they feel that these are the ones necessary to succeed in the business world.

MODIFYING 'A' TYPE BEHAVIOUR

> You grow up the day you have the first real laugh – at yourself.
>
> (Ethel Barrymore)

Here are some suggestions for easing back on 'A' type characteristics:

- Lighten up – you only live once. Live, love, let go and be happy. Learn to laugh at yourself – accept that everyone makes mistakes, including yourself. Remember:

  To err is human.

  (Alexander Pope)

- Don't limit your activities to work. Your family would probably appreciate your company, and time, more than seeing you completely wrapped up in your work or striving to bring home a fat income.

- Listen to other people's opinions and views without interrupting them, and value their differences.

- Praise other people, and praise yourself too – it's a great way of building self-esteem.

- Separate your work from other areas of your life.

- Trust other people and delegate. They might not do things as efficiently as you do, but give them a chance – you might be pleasantly surprised – and people appreciate being asked to help.

- Slow down – you move too fast. Give yourself a break before you break. Stop setting yourself such rigid deadlines. **Chill out!**

- Nurture yourself. Stop making impossible demands on yourself. Take life as it comes, instead of trying to control everything and everyone. Learn the value of relaxing and having fun, instead of always doing and striving.

- Take up an activity or hobby that is non-competitive.

- Build some unstructured time into each day.

- Learn to share your feelings.

- Work towards becoming a Hardy Personality (see Activity 4).

- Be hardy, hearty and healthy, instead of pressured, stressed out and wealthy.

One of the symptoms of approaching nervous breakdown is the belief that one's work is terribly important. If I were a medical man I should prescribe a holiday to any patient who considered his work important.

(Bertrand Russell)

CASE STUDY 5 – HARDY HANNAH

Hannah was a friendly young woman – not a lot 'ruffled her feathers'. People were always welcome in her home. She didn't worry if the house was a bit untidy. She believed people would far rather have the pleasure of her company than inspect her shelves for layers of dust. Hannah knew exactly where she was going in life. She wasn't overly ambitious – preferring to go with the flow of life. She accepted she had faults and could laugh at her mistakes. Hannah set herself realistic goals in life and steadily worked towards achieving them. If problems cropped up at work or in her relationships she would tackle them – never leaving things to fester. Hannah had the ability to take life as it comes. Hannah brought a lot of joy into other people's lives.

She was definitely not a hard-hearted Hannah – she possessed all the characteristics of a hardy and happy personality.

ACTIVITY 4 – Establishing whether you are a hardy personality

Can you take a lot of pressure without getting stressed out?
Tick the response which most fits your personality.

	Yes	No
Are you a friendly and outgoing person?	☐	☐
Is your manner and behaviour consistent?	☐	☐
Do you set yourself realistic and clearly defined goals?	☐	☐
Do you accept that you have faults?	☐	☐
Do you admit your mistakes?	☐	☐
Do you face up to your problems?	☐	☐
Do you take a problem-solving attitude to your difficulties?	☐	☐
Do you live in the present instead of dwelling on the past, or planning too far into the future?	☐	☐
Do you respond positively to change?	☐	☐
Do you feel fully committed to your work?	☐	☐
Do you take life as it comes, accepting its ups and downs?	☐	☐

Interpreting your scores

- If your Yes scores are high on this questionnaire it indicates that you possess a hardy personality and probably cope well with pressure.
- Check your No scores. These will give you pointers to areas you could do some work on to reduce the likelihood of stress.

SUMMARY OF HARDY PERSONALITIES

Hardy types are:

- easy going – they go with the flow of life
- patient, tolerant, calm, unflustered
- not easily irritated by other people

- able to give themselves time to think and reflect
- good at setting themselves realistic goals
- able to give and receive praise and affection easily
- adept at maintaining a healthy balance between work and play
- interested in hearing about what is happening in other people's lives.

ACTIVITY 5 – Working towards a more balanced lifestyle

Does your life look like this?   Or more like this?

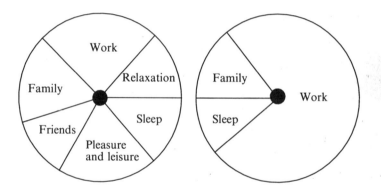

If your life looks more like the second pie chart you need to take action to get it more into balance. Consider the following questions:

1. What action can you take to create a more balanced lifestyle?

2. Why do you spend so much time working? Is it possible you use work as a way of avoiding facing up to difficulties in your personal life, or because you fear intimacy?

3. Do you hear your wife saying: 'I wish you would spend more time at home with me and the kids'? Do you reply with something like: 'I'm only working for you and the kids, dear, so you can have a better standard of living'?

Marriages often go adrift because the husband works long hours in the belief that it's his duty to provide the best he can for his wife and family, when all his wife really wants is for him to spend more time with her and the children.

ADDING THE FINISHING TOUCHES TO YOUR SELF-PICTURE

Every picture tells a story.

(Proverb)

Imagine it's time to enter your self-picture in a competition. Focus fully on what you have discovered about yourself from working through this chapter. Use your imagination, add a touch of inspiration, and a dash of perspiration, and put the finishing touches to your picture. Check out the following:

- Have you considered every angle that can lead you to success?
- Have you considered every strategy to help you thrive on stress?

IDENTIFYING STRESS SYMPTOMS YOU MUST TAKE SERIOUSLY

If you are experiencing any of the symptoms listed below, or a range of symptoms, you would be wise to seek professional help. Some of the symptoms may not necessarily be stress-related, but for your own peace of mind it's worth getting them checked out.

- If you feel unable to cope.
- If you feel depressed, anxious or panicky.
- If you are feeling helpless or hopeless.
- If you are getting heart palpitations or dizziness.
- If you get ringing in the ears (tinnitus).
- If you are suffering from blurred vision.
- If you are suffering from excessive fatigue or exhaustion.
- If you are experiencing:
  - frequent bouts of heartburn
  - frequent bouts of diarrhoea
  - difficulty in swallowing
  - stomach cramps

– recurring headaches or migraines.

- If you have lost your appetite.

- If you have lost your enthusiasm, energy and sparkle.

- If your thinking has become muddled, or you are having negative or irrational thoughts.

- If your sleep pattern is disturbed.

- If all the joy, fun and laughter has gone out of your life.

- If you are experiencing outbursts of anger or hostility.

- If you have lost your sex drive.

- If you have developed obsessions or compulsions.

- If you find it impossible to relax or switch off.

KEEPING YOUR PERSONAL DEVELOPMENT JOURNAL

If we had no faults we should not take so much pleasure in noticing them in others.

(Duc de la Rochefoucauld)

Reflect on what you have learnt about yourself by carrying out the activities in this chapter. Prepare a full stress profile of yourself. Include:

1. any areas of stress you have identified in your personal and working life, together with their causes and effects

2. any 'A' type characteristics you have identified you need to work on

3. a complete list of the strategies you have come up with to help you thrive on stress

4. a starting date for putting these strategies into action

5. one treat you will give yourself for all the hard work you have done by completing the activities in this chapter (**you deserve it**!).

Look well into thyself; there is a source of strength which will always spring up if thou wilt always look there.

(Marcus Aurelius)

3

Learning the Art of Relaxation

The first step is the hardest.

(Proverb)

UNDERSTANDING WHY RELAXATION IS SO IMPORTANT

The body and mind are inextricably linked. When our body feels relaxed our mind becomes calmer. Therefore, the first vital step in learning to thrive on stress is to master the art of relaxation.

Most of us know how to relax to some degree. But sometimes, because of the pressures of everyday living, we fail to relax when we most need to. There's more to relaxation than just simply sitting and watching television or listening to music. To become completely relaxed we need to let go of tension in our body and anxiety in our mind. This may be easier said than done. However, once you have learnt the art of relaxation it can be used effectively in any situation giving rise to stress or anxiety.

What happens when we feel anxious?

When we feel anxious, our muscles tense up. We may get a 'knotted' feeling in our stomach, scowl, clench our teeth, twist our legs tightly around each other, or feel tension in our neck and shoulders. This all uses up a great deal of muscular energy.

Why do we become tense and anxious?

To answer this question let us imagine a family scene.

CASE STUDY 6 – WOUND-UP WENDY AND LAID-BACK LAWRENCE

Wendy has recently returned to work after having a baby. Lawrence has two children by a previous marriage, Denise aged nine, and Mark aged seven. They are living with Wendy and Lawrence. Wendy is working five hours a day to fit in with the children's school hours. She leaves baby Rebecca with a childminder.

It is breakfast time

Wendy is rushing around dressing and feeding Rebecca, as well as getting breakfast for Lawrence, Denise and Mark. Lawrence has had a leisurely shower. He is sitting enjoying his breakfast and reading the newspaper. They both leave for work at 8.30 am, but prior to leaving Wendy has made the beds, washed up the breakfast dishes, prepared the children's lunches, quickly dusted round, and put the wheelie bin and milk bottles out.

Wendy feels wound-up – Lawrence is laid-back

Wendy bundles the kids in the car, ready to drop Rebecca off at the childminder's and Denise and Mark off at school. Lawrence and Wendy take the same route. There is a traffic jam on the entrance to the motorway. Wendy says to herself: (*mind-talk*) 'That's all I need!' This increases her frustration. She starts breathing fast and shallow and feels herself getting anxious. Lawrence, on the other hand, says to himself: (*mind-talk*) 'Oh well, there's no point in getting wound-up about it, there's nothing I can do'. He accepts the situation, remains calm, and listens to some music on the radio.

Wendy feels the pressure mounting

At 3.30 pm Wendy picks Denise and Mark up from school, and Rebecca from the childminder. She then goes shopping at the local supermarket, where she has to queue for ages at the checkout. She arrives home just after 5.00 pm feeling exhausted. While she is trying to unpack the shopping, Rebecca is screaming for a feed, and Denise and Mark are bickering and complaining about being hungry. Wendy feels her blood start to boil!

Lawrence keeps Wendy's blood on the simmer

Lawrence arrives home at 5.30 pm. He changes into jeans and a sweatshirt, sits in his favourite recliner, and flicks on the television with the remote control. He calls out to Wendy: 'How long will dinner be, love? I'm absolutely ravenous.'

Wendy stews in her own juices

Wendy bites her tongue and says nothing. She gets on and prepares the evening meal, feeds Rebecca and changes her nappy. After dinner she gives Rebecca a bath, settles her down for the night,

collects a pile of dirty washing and puts the washing machine on.
Denise and Mark go off to bed at 8.00 pm.

Wendy's mind starts working overtime
Wendy sits down at 8.15 pm, and tries to relax. The television is on
but she finds it impossible to concentrate on the programme because
she has a lot on her mind. She is thinking about all the things she has
to do tomorrow. She glances at Lawrence, who is enjoying his usual
evening catnap. She thinks to herself: (*mind-talk*) 'Bloody typical.
It's just not fair. I wish to God I'd been born a man.' This negative
mind-talk increases her feelings of frustration.

Wendy blows a gasket
When Lawrence stirs from his forty winks, Wendy explodes: 'I'm
absolutely sick of doing everything while you just sit there enjoying
life. You never lift a damn finger to help. You expect your dinner on
the table the minute you get in, and your bloody kids don't help
either. All I am is a slave to you lot. It's no wonder your first wife left
you. I wish I'd listened to my mother, she said I'd end up making a
rod for my own back.' (Wendy uses the fight response – albeit
inappropriately.)

Lawrence fights back
Lawrence retaliates with: 'I can't see what you're getting so worked
up about, love. The way you carry on anyone would think I did
nothing around here. You've got it made, just look at all the labour-
saving gadgets I've bought you – money doesn't grow on trees you
know. My poor old Mum would have loved all the appliances you've
got. My kids don't cause you much hassle, and you knew what you
were taking on when you married me. It's obviously working that's
getting to you and nobody forced you to go back to work – that was
your choice. You want to get a grip of yourself, love, or you'll give
yourself a heart attack.'

Wendy takes flight
Wendy thinks to herself: (*mind-talk*) 'What's the bloody point? He
never listens to a word I say.' She goes off to bed with a cauldron of
powerful negative emotions bubbling away inside her – she feels
hurt, angry, resentful, exasperated and despairing.

Lawrence gets the wrong end of the stick
Lawrence settles back in his recliner to watch a film. He thinks to

himself: (*mind-talk*) 'I'll never understand women. I don't know why they have to be so emotional. I guess it's something to do with their hormones. Still she'll get over it – she always does.' He goes to bed at midnight and snuggles up to Wendy. She pushes him away saying: 'Leave me alone, I've got a headache, and it's all your bloody fault.' **Get the picture?**

ACTION REPLAY

By slowing down the action, and replaying the scene, we can see that Wendy and Lawrence have got their wires well and truly crossed. Can you identify what is fuelling the fire between them?

- One of the biggest problems is poor communication. They are not hearing or listening to each other effectively. There is a lot of blaming and accusations. Lawrence makes assumptions about why Wendy is so wound-up, and also patronises her. In Chapter 6 (Communicating Skilfully) we will be revisiting them to see how different things look when they communicate effectively.

- Wendy's mind-talk is negative, which generates a lot of negative emotions. Chapter 4 addresses the important subject of how to challenge negative mind-talk.

- Wendy does not express her feelings. She bottles them up until she finally explodes – which proves counter-productive. Chapter 5 addresses how to express feelings effectively, and here we will see how Wendy is caught in the negative stress cycle.

- Wendy is showing a range of stress symptoms:
  - *Emotional* – anxiety, frustration, resentment, hurt, anger, exasperation and despair
  - *mental* – difficulty concentrating and negative thoughts
  - *behavioural* – difficulty relaxing
  - *physical* – fast and shallow breathing.

For the moment, let us concentrate on Wendy's physical symptoms – her fast and shallow breathing. This is an unhelpful way of breathing, which can produce a whole host of distressing symptoms. If Wendy learnt how to control her breathing, this would help her to calm herself down.

LEARNING TO BREATHE EFFECTIVELY

To begin with, let us look at what happens when we breathe normally (calmly and evenly). The pattern goes like this:

- We breathe approximately every six seconds.

- When we inhale, a fresh supply of oxygen is taken in from the air. This passes into the bloodstream, via our lungs. As it flows around the body it collects carbon dioxide (the waste products in the body).

- When we exhale, carbon dioxide is passed out of the bloodstream, via our lungs.

Each cell in our body needs to receive blood containing the correct amount of oxygen and carbon dioxide (gases) for it to function effectively. Providing our lungs are healthy, we are reasonably fit, and we breathe correctly, everything should be fine. However, if we start to **overbreathe** (too fast and too shallow) problems arise.

Identifying what triggers overbreathing and how it affects us

When we feel threatened, either physically or emotionally, we start to breathe a lot faster than usual. This happens as a result of adrenalin being passed into the bloodstream (which prepares us to fight the threat). If the threat is a physical one and we can respond to it physically (by adopting the fight response), this increased breathing rate is very useful to us. However, if the threat is on an emotional level, and the fight response is not appropriate, this increased breathing rate can leave us feeling very ill-at-ease. If we overbreathe for more than a few minutes we may start to feel very unwell, and begin to worry that there might be something seriously wrong with us.

Overbreathing disturbs the levels of oxygen and carbon dioxide in the bloodstream. Too much carbon dioxide is exhaled, which upsets the balance required for the cells in our body to operate efficiently. It affects our muscles, nerves, brain, eyes, heart and stomach. Although there is nothing physically wrong with us (which is often hard to believe) overbreathing can leave us feeling below par.

Overbreathing can become a habit

When we feel anxious we often breathe in this unhelpful way. Overbreathing can develop into a habit (*and habits are hard to break*). It can also set up a vicious cycle:

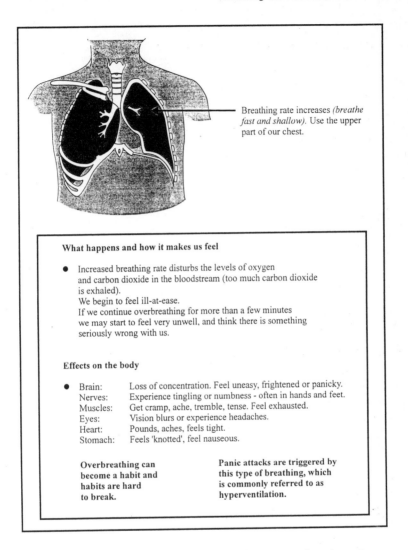

Breathing rate increases *(breathe fast and shallow)*. Use the upper part of our chest.

What happens and how it makes us feel

● Increased breathing rate disturbs the levels of oxygen and carbon dioxide in the bloodstream (too much carbon dioxide is exhaled).
We begin to feel ill-at-ease.
If we continue overbreathing for more than a few minutes we may start to feel very unwell, and think there is something seriously wrong with us.

Effects on the body

● Brain: Loss of concentration. Feel uneasy, frightened or panicky.
   Nerves: Experience tingling or numbness - often in hands and feet.
   Muscles: Get cramp, ache, tremble, tense. Feel exhausted.
   Eyes: Vision blurs or experience headaches.
   Heart: Pounds, aches, feels tight.
   Stomach: Feels 'knotted', feel nauseous.

Overbreathing can become a habit and habits are hard to break.

Panic attacks are triggered by this type of breathing, which is commonly referred to as hyperventilation.

Fig. 3. An overview of what happens when we overbreathe and how it affects us.

Feel threatened – overbreathe – brings on panicky feelings – breathe even faster – feel even more panicky... and so on.

Overbreathing is more commonly referred to as **hyperventilation**. Figure 3 gives an overview of what happens when we overbreathe, and how it affects us.

Panic attacks

Panic attacks are triggered by hyperventilation. One useful technique for restoring the equilibrium during a panic attack is to breathe into and out of a paper bag. The carbon dioxide exhaled into the bag is breathed back into the lungs. This restores the balance of oxygen and carbon dioxide in the body, which in turn reduces the sufferer's feelings of panic.

Effective breathing

The most effective type of breathing is abdominal breathing, which involves breathing slowly and gently from the lower part of our chest. Abdominal breathing reduces tension, anxiety and panic, and helps us feel more in control. It also aids relaxation. The following activity is designed to teach you how to breathe effectively from your abdominal area.

ACTIVITY 6 – Abdominal breathing

The most comfortable position for carrying out this activity is sitting in a chair that supports your arms and head. Don't restrict your breathing by folding your arms across your chest. Allow them to relax – either on the arms of the chair or on your lap. Make sure your neck feels relaxed. Close your eyes if this helps you feel more relaxed.

Are you sitting comfortably?

- Start by taking a gentle breath in through your nostrils, and then let it flow out again gently. Continue breathing in this relaxed way. Pay particular attention to how your chest expands and then sags down again. Follow the pattern in your mind.

- Try to ensure that the flow of movement only takes place in the lower part of your chest (your abdominal area) – see Figure 4. To check whether you are doing this correctly, place one hand on the upper part of your chest and the other on your abdomen. Follow the flow of movement. If you are breathing from your abdomen the upper part of your chest should feel relaxed and still.

- As you breathe in through your nostrils, feel the oxygen filling the empty space in your lungs. When you breathe out feel how the space in your chest reduces as the carbon dioxide flows out of

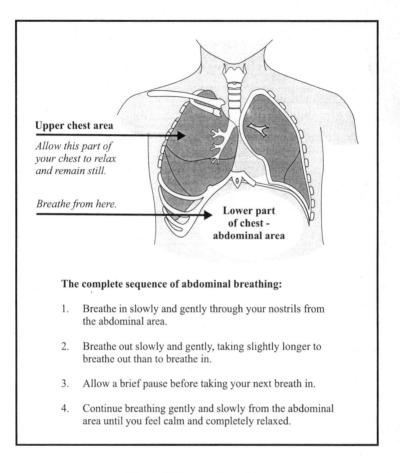

Fig. 4. Abdominal breathing.

your lungs. Take slightly longer to breathe out than to breathe in. Each time you breathe out, allow a brief pause before taking in your next breath. There is no need to rush. Enjoy the feeling of calm. Continue breathing *gently* and *slowly* from your abdomen, following the flow of movement in your mind, until you feel completely relaxed.

Practise abdominal breathing regularly. Eventually it will become automatic, and you won't need to think about it. Remember to keep your arms and neck relaxed. You will probably notice as you become more proficient that your arms and neck will feel more relaxed, which in turn will help you breathe even more effectively.

Note: Abdominal breathing can be practised anywhere – sitting in a traffic jam, before an important exam, in the middle of a difficult meeting. Nobody need see you breathing, and silently adding the words 'calm down' or 'relax' to yourself as you breathe out can bring immediate relief from tension, anxiety and panic.

MASTERING THE ART OF RELEASING TENSION

Muscular relaxation training helps relieve tension. Below I set out the sequence for mastering the art of releasing tension and how to apply it to 15 major muscle groups. The best position to practise is lying down. Try this brief exercise first.

- Clench your right fist tightly. Hold it in this position for six seconds. Slowly release your fingers, open them out and let your hand go limp. Notice the difference between tension and relaxation?

Sequence
Focus...tense...hold for a count of six...release...relax.

What to do
1. **Forehead**
   Wrinkle forehead by raising eyebrows as high as possible.
2. **Eye-brow and eye-lids**
   Frown as hard as possible and squeeze eyes shut.
3. **Nose**
   Wrinkle nose
4. **Lips and face**
   Press lips tightly together.
5. **Tongue and throat**
   Push tongue against roof of mouth.
6. **Jaw**
   Bite teeth hard together.
7. **Neck and throat**
   Pull chin down hard towards chest without it actually touching chest.
8. **Shoulders**

Shrug shoulders hard.
9. **Chest**
   Pull shoulder blades together.
10. **Biceps (front upper arms)**
    Bend arms to shoulders with wrists.
12. **Triceps (back upper arms)**
    Straighten arms as hard as possible.
12. **Stomach**
    Tighten muscles as though you are preparing to receive a blow.
13. **Hips and lower back**
    Squeeze buttocks together.
14. **Hands and lower arms**
    Clench fists and tense muscles in lower arms.
15. **Legs and feet**
    Straighten legs pointing toes downwards. Pull toes back towards head.

PREPARING FOR A RELAXATION SESSION

The environment

Make sure the room in which you are going to practise is warm and quiet, and that you won't be disturbed. If necessary, unplug the telephone for an hour. Dim the lights. If the time you have available is limited, it might be advisable to have an alarm clock nearby, set to wake you up in half an hour, in case you achieve a deep state of relaxation.

Clothing

Remove any tight clothing – for example, ties, belts – and remove shoes, glasses, contact lenses and bulky items of jewellery.

Timing

Allow yourself half an hour to complete your relaxation routine and set this amount of time aside each day to continue practising. If you suffer from insomnia, it can be particularly useful to practise relaxing during the evening.

Position

The most beneficial position for relaxing is lying down, either on a bed or lying on the floor on a soft mat or carpet. Have two pillows available, one to place under your head and shoulders, and one under your knees. However, if lying down is uncomfortable, the routines can be done sitting in a firm chair that supports your head, back and arms, and allows you to rest your feet on the floor. Whether you are lying or sitting, allow your arms and hands to rest on a comfortable surface.

Carrying out the routines
Until you are familiar with the routines, ask someone to read them out to you. Alternatively, record the instructions on an audio cassette, and play the tape back to yourself. You are given a choice of two routines. Routine 1 is a muscular relaxation exercise. Routine 2 is a deep relaxation exercise. Follow the instructions for each carefully.

Warming up
- To begin with, ensure that your head is in a comfortable position.

- Close your eyes.

- Arrange your arms and legs in a comfortable position. Your legs should be about 18 inches apart with your feet turned outwards. The palms of your hands should be facing upwards, with fingers open and relaxed.

- Practise your breathing pattern until you feel calm and at peace.

- Allow your mind to clear itself of all thoughts except about letting your body relax.

ACTIVITY 7 – Relaxation routine 1

Sequence: Push...release...notice the difference.
Note: After every push hold for a count of six...release slowly... and relax.

Start by pushing your **eyebrows** upwards towards your hairline. Hold for a count of six.

NOTICE
How your forehead smooths out as you release.

With your **eyes** closed, eyelids relaxed and head still:

Push your eyes upwards.
Push your eyes downwards.
Push your eyes to the right.
Push your eyes to the left.

How relaxed your
eyelids become and
your eyes beneath
them.

Push your **lips** gently and
evenly together, and push
your lower jaw down.
Push your **tongue** down away
from the roof of your mouth.

How relaxed the
lower part of your
face becomes.

Move down to your **shoulders**.
Push both shoulders down-
wards towards your feet.

How the tension
flows out of your
shoulders.

Move to your **elbows**. Gently
push them out to the side
and slightly raise them.

How the tension
leaves your elbows.

Move to your **hands**. Push
your fingers outwards and as
wide as you can.

How loose your
fingers feel.

Move to your **hips**. Push your
hips so they roll outwards.

How the tension
leaves your hips.

Push your **knees** (one at a
time) so they straighten and
your heel lifts off the floor.

How your legs
become looser.

Push your **ankles** at the upper
part of your foot so your foot
is pushed downwards to the
floor.

How each ankle
becomes looser.

Push the curve of your **back**
into the floor.

How your stomach
muscles relax.

This is the end of relaxation routine 1.

ACTIVITY 8 – Deep relaxation, routine 2

Sequence: Tell each group of muscles to let go and relax.

Remember to breathe from your abdomen before starting the relaxation routine.

Start by telling all the muscles of your body to let go and relax. *Repeat – let go and relax – let go and relax.*

Focus on the muscles of your **forehead**. Tell all the muscles of your forehead to let go and relax. *Repeat – let go and relax – let go and relax.*

Focus on the muscles of your **eyes**. Tell all the muscles of your eyes to let go and relax. *Repeat – let go and relax – let go and relax.*

Focus on the muscles of your **face**. Tell all the muscles of your face to let go and relax. *Repeat – let go and relax – let go and relax.*

Focus on the muscles of your **neck**. Tell all the muscles of your neck to let go and relax. *Repeat – let go and relax – let go and relax.*

Focus on the muscles of your **shoulders**. Tell all the muscles of your shoulders to let go and relax. *Repeat – let go and relax – let go and relax.*

Focus on the muscles of your **arms**. Tell all the muscles of your arms to let go and relax. *Repeat – let go and relax – let go and relax.*

Focus on the muscles

of your **hands**. Tell all the
muscles of your hands
to let go and relax.   *Repeat – let go and relax – let go and relax.*

Focus on the muscles
of your **back**. Tell all the
muscles of your back
to let go and relax.   *Repeat – let go and relax – let go and relax.*

Focus on the muscles
of your **stomach**. Tell all
the muscles of your
stomach to let go and
relax.   *Repeat – let go and relax – let go and relax.*

Focus on the muscles
of your **buttocks**. Tell all
the muscles of your
buttocks to let go and
relax.   *Repeat – let go and relax – let go and relax.*

Focus on the muscles
of your **thighs**. Tell all the
muscles of your thighs
to let go and relax.   *Repeat – let go and relax – let go and relax.*

Focus on the muscles
of your **feet**. Tell all the
muscles of your feet
to let go and relax.   *Repeat – let go and relax – let go and relax.*

Focus on the muscles
of your **forehead, eyes,
face, neck, shoulders,
arms, hands, back,
stomach, buttocks,
thighs, calves** and **feet**.
Tell all the muscles
of your body to
let go and relax.   *Repeat – let go and relax – let go and relax.*

In this relaxed position use your imagination to create a picture in your mind. Take yourself to your favourite place – a beach – a river – wherever you feel happy and at peace. Take in the sounds and smells around you. When you have savoured the mental image you have created for yourself sit up very slowly...take your time....there's no need to rush.

Let your mind wander and take you to a place of peace and tranquillity.

MONITORING PROGRESS

In your personal development journal design a relaxation log similar to the example in Figure 5, to enable you to keep track of your progress.

ACTIVITY 9 – Relaxing mentally

When we feel tense or anxious it affects our ability to concentrate. Focusing your complete attention on a fixed object for five minutes, such as a lighted candle or vase of flowers, is a constructive way of quietening your mind. Sit totally still, taking in every detail of the object – its colours, its texture, its shape. At the end of five minutes, close your eyes for a few moments and then continue with whatever you were doing before.

EXPLORING OTHER STRESS RELIEVING TECHNIQUES

1. Alternative therapies

There are many alternative therapies which can help relieve symptoms of stress and anxiety. Here are some of them:

Scoring: 10 = very tense. 1 = very relaxed.

Day/Date	Before relaxation	After relaxation	Comments on the day in general
Example 1.3.9X	8	3	Felt tense after attending a difficult meeting. Carried out deep relaxation exercise. Still slightly tense afterwards.

Fig. 5. Example of a relaxation log.

- acupressure – also referred to as Shiatsu
- acupuncture
- Alexander Technique
- aromatherapy
- Bach Flower Healing
- head and shoulder massage
- hypnotherapy
- massage
- Reiki Healing
- reflexology.

2. Autogenic Training (AT)

Autogenics is a series of mental exercises which reduce stress and encourage relaxation. Dr John M. English, an autogenic trainer at Salisbury, Wiltshire, says about AT:

> The relaxation exercises are taken from the sort of talk hypnotists used to relax clients at the turn of the century: phrases suggesting warmth and heaviness in various parts of the body, and peacefulness. AT instruction is systematised into 6 'standard exercises' normally taught over 8 weekly sessions, in a group, or more flexibly for individuals. Experience shows that the exercises are potent, and there are reactions to doing them, which would not be understood, or properly handled by untrained individuals. We therefore prefer that people do not experiment themselves, but do the course properly.

3. Biofeedback

Biofeedback involves the use of electronic instruments to measure muscle tension, heart rate, blood pressure, brain wave activity, skin temperature and sweat gland activity. It demonstrates which components of the nervous system are relaxed and which are not. Used alone, it does not bring about relaxation. Physical and mental relaxation strategies are used in conjunction with the treatment.

4. Counselling

If stress is due to emotional problems, working through the problems with a qualified counsellor can help to reduce the symptoms.

5. Exercise

Aerobic exercise ('with air'), performed regularly, can reduce the risk of heart disease, help with weight control, and also have positive psychological effects; for example, improved self-esteem, reduced anxiety and relief from depression. Aerobic exercises include walking briskly, aerobic dancing, running, swimming, cycling and rowing.

6. Meditation

Meditation focuses the mind, encouraging a passive attitude which decreases muscular tension.

7. Nutrition

Eating the right food is vital for healthy bodily functioning. A healthy diet should include foods such as fruits, vegetables and grains which are high in carbohydrates and fibre, low in fat and free from cholesterol. These should make up about 50 per cent of your daily calorie intake. The remainder should come from low-fat dairy produce, fish, poultry and lean meats. Needless to say, excessive alcohol consumption should be avoided.

8. Yoga

Yoga involves learning a series of mental and physical exercises which calm the mind and aid relaxation.

If you decide to pursue any of the stress-relieving approaches suggested here, be sure to consult a qualified practitioner. Stress management is now big business, so beware of charlatans. Your best route is to consult your GP, local hospital or health clinic. For details of training courses in any of the techniques, contact your local adult education centre or university.

Carrying out daily relaxation exercises can help to alleviate stress symptoms. However, do not stop taking any medication prescribed by your GP, without first seeking his or her advice.

KEEPING YOUR PERSONAL DEVELOPMENT JOURNAL

One hour's sleep before midnight is worth two after.

(Proverb)

1. Record the complete sequence for effective breathing.

2. Record the sequence for releasing muscular tension.

3. Record which stress-relieving techniques appeal to you most.

4. Look through your local *Yellow Pages* under Therapists. Note how many different types of therapies are listed. Record how you would go about checking a therapist's qualifications.

5. Make a note of things you do at the moment to help you relax; for example, listening to music, reading, gardening.

6. Make a list of other things you would like to do that could help you relax.

Something attempted, something done,
has earned a night's repose.

(Longfellow)

4

Eliminating Negative Mind-talk

A strong positive mental attitude will create more miracles
than any wonder drug.

(Patricia Neal)

Mastering the art of relaxing our body can be of tremendous value
in relieving the physical symptoms of stress. The next important
stage in learning to thrive on stress is to gain awareness into what
goes on in our mind, and to learn how to become masters of our own
mind. This involves 'tuning into' what we are telling our mind (**mind-
talk**), and eliminating negative mind-talk. Negative messages fed to
the mind have a powerful effect on our body, frame of mind and
behaviour. They tend to weigh us down and put us in a **sad or sorry
frame of mind**, which leads to negative feelings and self-defeating
behaviour. Positive mind-talk, on the other hand, lifts our mood. It
puts us in a **happy frame of mind**, which energises the body, and
results in positive action.

What exactly is mind-talk?
All of us talk silently in our minds (our private unspoken thoughts).
We are constantly having a running commentary about what
happened to us in the past, what is happening to us in the present,
and what might happen to us in the future. Psychologists refer to
this as 'self-talk'. I prefer to call it 'mind-talk', because it is my belief
that everything happens in the mind – **that the silent voice is in fact
our mind talking**. To understand this silent voice a bit better let us
take a look at what goes on in the mind.

UNDERSTANDING WHAT GOES ON IN THE MIND

One way of looking at the mind is to view it as the centre of
operations. The mind is a highly complex system which contains our

thoughts, feelings, memories, recall, beliefs, values, attitude, judgement, intellect, will, wit, wishes and desires, sense, sentiment, imagination (our mind's eye), *etc.* **It's all in the mind**.

Our thoughts are shaped by the contents of the mind

Every thought starts in our mind, is processed by the mind, and is shaped by the contents of the mind. Before a thought leaves the mind (if it does), it goes through a complicated process.

Let us view this process as:

- the thought processor.

The thought processor then searches the contents of the mind seeking out information before deciding what action to take on the thought. Let us view this process as:

- the mind researcher.

Example
Imagine you have been divorced and are thinking about getting remarried, and that silent voice (your mind-talk) is debating the ifs and buts (chewing things over in your mind).

The mind researcher decides:

- To call in on your **memories** – who say:
  'I'm not sure – **remember** *– it didn't work out last time!'*

- It then calls in on your **feelings** – who say:
  'It caused me a lot of pain and grief when my first marriage ended.'

- It then calls in on your **beliefs** – who say:
  'It **must** *have been my fault the marriage failed. I* **should** *have tried harder. I'm not marriage material. I'm a failure.'*

- Finally, it calls in on your **imagination** (your mind's eye) – who says:
  'I can **visualise** *it all going wrong again* (**predicting the future** – **as if you have a crystal ball**) *and that would be* **disastrous**. *I* **can't** *take the risk.'*

The mind researcher then collates all these messages (mind-talk) and feeds its findings back to the thought processor, who either:

1. Processes the thoughts into verbal communication via the word processor (the mouth), which externalises the thoughts.

2. Sends the thoughts to the back of the mind and hopes they will go away (out of sight – out of mind). This often happens if we are having conflicting thoughts; for example if we cannot make up our mind or are in two minds about something.

3. Decides that the thoughts are too distressing to think about or deal with (the mind cannot cope with them). So it locks the thoughts away (together with the associated painful feelings) in a safe vault in the deepest recesses of the memory of the mind, and hopes they will never resurface. Here they gather dust, fade, and over time may get distorted – **but they never do go away completely**.

   This often happens when someone has suffered a horrific trauma such as childhood sexual abuse, physical or emotional abuse, rape, severe neglect or deprivation. However, the thoughts and feelings may show themselves in disguised form (for example, as depression and anxiety) or in behaviour (for example, self-harm). They can also be reactivated by a further traumatic experience (for example, childbirth) or by the senses – a smell (for example, a particular aftershave), or a sound (for example, a voice similar to the abuser's).

   People who have experienced horrendous traumas are in psychological pain and need professional counselling or psychotherapy. With the right help and support they can start to heal by unlocking the memory vaults of their mind, verbalising their thoughts, and externalising their inner suffering.

IDENTIFYING THE EFFECTS OF NEGATIVE THOUGHTS

Negative thoughts don't go away. They keep popping up in our mind. They haunt us, torment us, until we end up dwelling on them. And that silent voice never stops droning on and on: *'Put your mind to it. Haven't you got a mind of your own? Are you out of your tiny mind? You must be off your trolley. Have you taken leave of your senses? Get on and make a decision. You're hopeless, stupid, useless, pathetic.'* Its constant nagging can put our mind into overdrive, make our thoughts race, and we end up having difficulty thinking straight.

- *Negative thoughts affect our body.* We begin to feel physically exhausted.

- *Negative thoughts affect our mood and emotions (our frame of mind).* We feel mentally drained and can't concentrate. We feel as if we are carrying the weight of the world on our shoulders. We can't stop worrying and the more we worry the worse it gets – the heavier the burden becomes.

- *Negative thoughts affect our behaviour.* We can't relax, we can't sleep, we pace the floor at night. We can't eat, or we scoff chocolate to comfort ourselves. We may smoke more than usual in the misguided belief that this will calm our mind down, or resort to alcohol or drugs to try and numb the mind.

- *Negative thoughts can hurl our mind into confusion and chaos.* Persistent negative thoughts can throw our mind into a complete turmoil, to the point where we begin to feel as if we are going out of our mind. Sadly, if these thoughts are not recognised and challenged, the end result can indeed be a mental breakdown.

Garbage in – garbage out

Those of you familiar with computer terminology may have come across the term **garbage in – garbage out (GIGO)**. What this basically means is that the computer is only as good as its operator. In other words, if garbage is fed into the computer, the outcome is gobbledegook. This links with my view of the mind, *ie* if we feed it with negative mind-talk, we get negative output in the way of negative feelings and self-defeating behaviour. Figure 6 summarises what goes on in the mind.

> I must have a prodigious quantity of mind; it takes me as much
> as a week, sometimes, to make it up.
>
> (Mark Twain)

BECOMING MASTERS OF OUR OWN MIND

Many of us carry rigid beliefs in our mind that we take on board from our parents or other significant authority figures. 'A' Type Alan (Case Study 4 in Chapter 2) provides us with an example of this. You may recall his parents saying to him:

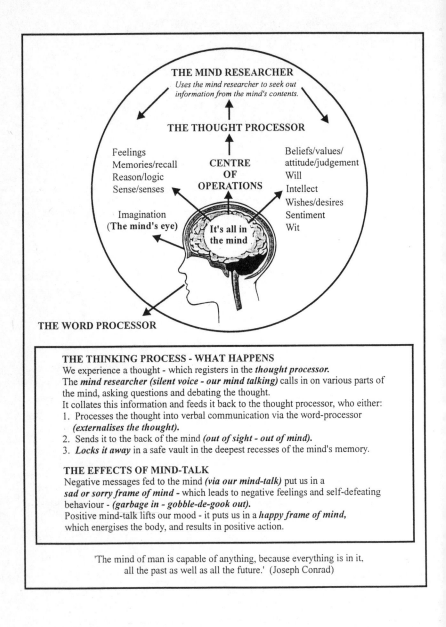

THE MIND RESEARCHER
*Uses the mind researcher to seek out
information from the mind's contents.*

THE THOUGHT PROCESSOR

Feelings
Memories/recall
Reason/logic
Sense/senses

CENTRE
OF
OPERATIONS

Beliefs/values/
attitude/judgement
Will
Intellect
Wishes/desires
Sentiment
Wit

Imagination
(The mind's eye)

It's all in
the mind

THE WORD PROCESSOR

THE THINKING PROCESS - WHAT HAPPENS
We experience a thought - which registers in the ***thought processor.***
The ***mind researcher (silent voice - our mind talking)*** calls in on various parts of
the mind, asking questions and debating the thought.
It collates this information and feeds it back to the thought processor, who either:
1. Processes the thought into verbal communication via the word-processor
   (externalises the thought).
2. Sends it to the back of the mind *(out of sight - out of mind).*
3. *Locks it away* in a safe vault in the deepest recesses of the mind's memory.

THE EFFECTS OF MIND-TALK
Negative messages fed to the mind *(via our mind-talk)* put us in a
sad or sorry frame of mind - which leads to negative feelings and self-defeating
behaviour - *(garbage in - gobble-de-gook out).*
Positive mind-talk lifts our mood - it puts us in a *happy frame of mind,*
which energises the body, and results in positive action.

'The mind of man is capable of anything, because everything is in it,
all the past as well as all the future.' (Joseph Conrad)

Fig. 6. Understanding what goes on in the mind.

- 'Surely you could have done better than that.'

- 'You really **must** try harder if you want to succeed like your father.'

Alan took these beliefs on board as:

I **must** succeed at all costs.
I **must** win.
I **must** strive for perfection.

Alan's self-esteem (his opinion of himself) was built on these beliefs, and as long as he succeeded and achieved, his self-esteem remained intact. However, when he lost a major case, he took this as a sign that he had failed. It shattered his self-esteem, which was already fragile as a result of feeling rejected and unloved in childhood.

We will be looking more at the subject of self-esteem and self-worth in Chapter 7. For the moment, though, let us try and imagine what Alan might have been saying to himself. It may well have gone something like this:

'It's all my fault. This is absolutely dreadful. I'm a failure. I'm useless – it's no wonder my parents don't love me. They'll never speak to me again. I can't face them – face anyone. I **should** *have tried harder. I* **ought to** *have spent longer preparing. I'll never be as successful as my father. I* **can't** *cope.'*

Feeding our mind with negative messages like these can lead to anguish and self-defeating behaviour which, as we saw, is exactly what happened to Alan.

Identifying what Alan could have said that might have changed the scenario

Let us look at how different things might have been if Alan had 'tuned into' that silent voice, and challenged the negative messages he was feeding his mind.

'I've had an excellent track record up until now, and it's unrealistic to expect to win every case. I presented the facts to the best of my ability, and that is all I can do. The jury made their decision based on the evidence, not on my performance, and it's not about winning – it's about justice. It's not the end of the world, and I've learnt a lot from it. I may not have succeeded in

this case, but that does not make **me** *a failure. I'm not going to let it get to me – life's too short to keep worrying about what everyone else thinks.'*

Sound different?

How Alan achieved his path to individuality

Before we leave Alan, there's another very significant point worth mentioning here. He did not choose his own career – he went along with what his parents considered was best for him, **believing** he had no right to question **their beliefs**. However, through therapy, he did start to question their beliefs, and recognised that what they thought was right for him, wasn't right for him. By separating his beliefs from his parents' beliefs, Alan was able to follow his path to individuality – he became master of his own mind and master of his own destiny. **Are you master of yours?**

No man should part with his own individuality and become that of another.

(Channing)

Clearing out the garbage

To begin to become masters of our mind we need to clear out the garbage messages we feed it. This includes disposing of any rigid beliefs we have 'inherited', that are no longer appropriate to us today. But how do we know if these beliefs are someone else's? The answer is to 'tune into' what you are saying to yourself – to listen to the silent words carefully, and to try and separate which beliefs are yours and which don't belong to you.

Separating beliefs

To separate your beliefs, ask yourself the following questions:

- Is this my belief?
- Is this the real me speaking?
- Am I carrying a parent or someone else around on my shoulder?
- Is this what they would have said?

It might help to write down your answers.

Examples

My belief is:	*Their belief was:*

- If I say 'No' people will think I am selfish.
- You should always put other people's needs first.

- I am useless.
- You will never make anything of yourself.

- I must always be strong.
- Only weak people show their feelings.

- I should keep the house spotless.
- An untidy house means an untidy mind.

Updating beliefs

If you identify any inherited beliefs, ask yourself:

- Is this belief helping me succeed today?
- Is carrying this belief creating stress in my life?
- Does this belief need updating? How?
- Does carrying this belief help or hinder me?

If you consider it is hindering you, try updating it.

Examples

My belief was:	*Updated belief:*

- If I say 'no' people will think I am selfish.
- It's OK to consider my own needs.
- I am useless.
- I am good at... A, B and C.
- I must always be strong.
- It's OK to be vulnerable.
- I should keep the house spotless.
- People feel more relaxed in a house that's lived in.

The quality of your thoughts determines the quality of your life.

(Vera Peiffer)

Identifying mind-talk menaces

There are certain damaging mind-talk words that can point to 'inherited' beliefs. These words are absolute menaces. Here are a few of them:

- should
- must
- got to
- ought to.

They imply a sense of duty or obligation, and create self-pressure. If we don't do our *shoulds, musts, got to's* or *ought to's*, we often give ourselves a hard time, or feel guilty or anxious because we haven't done them.

Examples
1. I **should** clean the kitchen cupboards.

2. I **must** mow the lawn.

3. I've **got to** get this assignment finished.

4. I **ought to** visit my neighbour.

Should shrinkers
By eliminating the word **should** from your mind-talk and replacing it with **could** you will notice how self-pressure starts to shrink away.

Example
1. I **could** clean the kitchen cupboards.

Could *gives us a choice. We can do it if we* **choose** *to*.

Must busters
By eliminating the word **must** from your mind-talk and replacing it with **will** you will notice how self-pressure minimises.

Example
2. I **will** mow the lawn.

The word **will** is a self-motivating word.

Got to grinders
By eliminating the words **got to** from your mind-talk and replacing them with **would like to** you will stop grinding yourself down.

Example
3. I **would like to** finish this assignment by the end of the week.

Would like to are self-motivating words which greatly ease self-pressure.

Ought to ousters
By ousting the words **ought to** from your mind-talk and replacing them with **want to** you will notice how self-pressure oozes away.

Example
4. I **want to** visit my neighbour.

Want to are self-motivating words, they spur you on to positive action.

ACTIVITY 10 – Pinpointing and replacing your mind-talk menaces

- **Shrinking your shoulds**. Think of four things you have been saying to yourself that you **should do**. Write them down.

- **Busting your musts**. Think of four things you have been telling yourself you **must do**. Write them down.

- **Grinding your got to's**. Think of four things you have been telling yourself you have **got to do**. Write them down.

- **Ousting your ought to's**. Think of four things you have been telling yourself you **ought to do**. Write them down.

Now consider why you haven't done them.

- Is it because you don't really want to do them?
- Is it an 'inherited' should, must, have got to, ought to do them?
- How do you feel about not having done them?

Replacing the menaces with mind-talk masters
Rewrite your list using mind-talk masters such as **could, will, would like to, want to, don't want to** – whatever words feel right for you. When you have rewritten your list reflect on whether you feel any different. Has it eased the self-pressure?

Catching your mind-talk menaces

- Every time you catch yourself silently using these damaging mind-talk menaces, challenge them with mind-talk masters. You will soon notice a difference in how you feel.

- Observe, too, how many times you hear other people verbalising these words in the course of a day, whether it's in the form of: 'I should/must', 'You should/must', or 'What you should/must do is'. It's a very interesting exercise.

Naturally, there are things we all have to do that we would prefer not to do. However, changing our mind-talk menaces into mind-talk masters can help us to face them in a more positive frame of mind.

Cancelling your can'ts

The word **can't** is another absolute menace. It puts obstacles in our way. Consider what you really mean when you are telling yourself you can't, and whether you are being strictly truthful with yourself. Do you really mean 'I don't want to', or 'I'm afraid to'?

ACTIVITY 11 – Cancelling your can'ts

Think of all the things you have been telling yourself you **can't do**, and then cancel them from your mind-talk by creating positive challenges.

Examples

I **can't** possibly do that.	I **can** have a go.
I **can't** let her down.	I **can** tell her I am too busy at the moment.

Recognising other mind-talk menaces

- **Yes ... but**. When we use the words 'yes...but' we are putting obstacles in our way again. Saying *'I will give it a go'* is more self-empowering and increases self-confidence.

- **I'm not good enough** ... leaves us feeling powerless and inadequate. Saying *'I am a worthwhile person'* is more self-empowering and increases self-confidence.

- **It was awful, dreadful, disastrous** ... leaves us stuck in the past.

Saying *'It was part of life's rich learning experience'* helps us move forward.

- **It's a problem**... keeps us stuck in the problem. Saying *'It's a learning opportunity'* motivates us to solve the problem.

Summarising the effects of mind-talk menaces
Mind-talk menaces tend to:

- Make situations seem worse than they really are.

- Keep us stuck in the past (*that's how it was*), and predict the future (*that's how it will always be*).

- Put obstacles in our way.

- Generate negative feelings which leads to self-defeating behaviour.

- Invite stress and depression, and reduce our ability to relax.

ACTIVITY 12 – Changing mind-talk menaces to mind-talk masters

Look at the mind-talk masters in the box below. See if you can work out which mind-talk master challenges each mind-talk menace, and write them alongside their corresponding menace.

Menace	Master		Menace	Master	
I must	(	)	I should	(	)
I can't	(	)	I need	(	)
It's not fair	(	)	It was awful	(	)
It's a problem	(	)	Yes...but	(	)
Life's a bitch	(	)	I might	(	)
I'm useless	(	)	I'm a failure	(	)
I can't cope	(	)	I'm not good enough	(	)
I'm stupid	(	)	I never have any luck	(	)

Mind-talk masters

I'm as good as the next person

I will   I can/won't

Who says so? Where's the evidence?

I could   I would like

It was regrettable

It's the way it is   Life is what I make it

I make my own luck

It's a challenge   I am going to

Just because I failed at... doesn't mean I'm a failure

Perhaps I could...   I'm a fallible human being

I feel confident I can handle it

Refer to the last page of this chapter to see if you have worked them out correctly.

Note: whenever you hear yourself saying I'm useless, hopeless, worthless – ask yourself: Who says so? Where's the evidence?

EXAMINING MIND-TALK IN ACTION

Let us now 'tune into' Negative Nellie and Positive Polly to see how two different women might handle the same scenario.

CASE STUDY 7 – NEGATIVE NELLIE

To be wronged is nothing unless you continue to remember it.

(Confucius)

Situation

Nellie's husband has left her for another woman. Nellie's mind-talk goes like this:

'It's just not fair. Still, I guess that's the story of my life. Some people have all the luck, but not me, nothing ever works out right. I suppose I am just one of life's losers. I did everything to please

Norman, now just look what he's gone and done – the swine. It's all right Caroline suggesting that I'd probably feel better if I got a job, but why the hell should I? Besides, who's going to give me a job without any qualifications? I gave up everything for Norman, and just look at the way he's treated me. It's awful. It's all his fault this has happened. I'll make the swine pay if it's the last thing I do. I wish to God I'd never met him.'

Identifying the underlying feelings and the likely outcome

As we can see, Nellie's mind-talk leaves her feeling very unhappy, victimised and resentful (*negative feelings*). She is placing the entire blame for the break-up on Norman, without giving any thought to her part in it, which leaves her wallowing in self-pity. It's possible that the thought of getting a job without having any qualifications is producing *fear*, but she is using *anger* to cover the fear. She is determined to seek revenge, regardless of the cost. If Nellie continues to feed her mind with these negative messages the chances are she will be the one to pay the highest price – she's already well on the road to stress and depression (self-defeating behaviour).

CASE STUDY 8 – POSITIVE POLLY

It takes two to make a quarrel

(Proverb)

Situation

Polly's husband has left her for another woman. Polly's mind-talk goes like this:

'I feel really sad that our marriage is over. However, it's no good dwelling on the past, life goes on. Just because it didn't work out with Norman, it doesn't mean to say I won't meet someone else I can be happy with. We both made our fair share of mistakes. I'll put it down to experience and won't make the same mistakes in the future. Caroline's suggestion about getting a job seems like a good idea. It will give me something else to think about. It might be difficult to get a job because I haven't got any qualifications. However, perhaps I could start by doing some voluntary work, or getting myself some training. I think I will make some enquiries.'

Identifying the underlying feelings and the likely outcome

Here we can see that Polly's mind-talk is self-empowering. She acknowledges her feelings of sadness, and is not placing the blame for the break-up entirely on Norman's shoulders. She accepts that it takes two to tango, and is willing to learn from her mistakes. She is determined not to stay stuck in the past, and is prepared to forgive and forget. She is not harbouring resentment, and is optimistic and realistic about the future. She takes action to improve the future. Polly's mind-talk is rational, it generates positive feelings and motivates her to take positive action.

MASTERING OUR MIND BY ELIMINATING THE MENACES

> The highest possible stage in moral culture is when we recognise that we ought to control our thoughts.
>
> (Charles Robert Darwin)

To eliminate mind-talk menaces there is a series of steps we need to take:

1. First, we need to become aware of the menaces by listening to the silent voice.

2. Second, we need to monitor our feelings. Often we experience a negative feeling first, and may not be aware that the feeling is a direct result of what we are saying in our mind. If this happens it helps to say: 'What have I been saying that is making me feel this way?' Negative feelings are a sure sign that we have been feeding our mind with negative messages.

3. Third, we need to challenge mind-talk menaces and replace them with mind-talk masters.

Challenging mind-talk menaces
To challenge mind-talk menaces effectively it helps to remember the following formula:

- **Catch the menaces:**   'What am I saying in my mind?'

- **Analyse the menaces:**   'Is what I'm saying in my mind influenced by anyone from the past?'

- **Challenge the menaces:**   'What could I say that would produce a more positive outcome?'

Summarising the effects of mind-talk masters
Mind-talk masters are different because they:

- put things into perspective – they don't make a drama out of a crisis
- don't predict the future
- help us succeed
- create positive outcomes
- protect us from stress and depression, and increase our ability to relax.

ACTIVITY 13 – Challenging Desperate Dan's mind-talk menaces

Read through Dan's silent mind-talk, and challenge his menaces with mind-talk masters.

Situation:
Dan has been invited to attend a job interview. His mind-talk goes like this:

'It's going to be a complete waste of time going. I'm probably too old, and I expect all the other applicants are better qualified than me. I've always been useless at interviews, and I'll probably ask all the wrong questions. No doubt they are interviewing a lot of people so I don't stand a chance.'

ACTIVITY 14 – Challenging your own mind-talk menaces

Think about a situation in your life that is currently causing you stress. Write a description of the situation.

Now try and get in touch with any mind-talk menaces that could be contributing to your stress. Write these menaces down.

Next try and get in touch with the feelings these menaces are generating in you. Write them down.

Now ask yourself the following questions:

1. Am I predicting the future negatively?   Yes/No
2. Am I making the situation worse than it really is?   Yes/No
3. Are these mind-talk menaces making me feel bad?   Yes/No
4. Are these mind-talk menaces helping me resolve
    the situation?   Yes/No

Replacing the menaces with mind-talk masters
Write down what you could say to challenge these self-defeating menaces.

Now ask yourself the following question:

> Has challenging my mind-talk menaces put me in a more positive frame of mind? If it has, utilise this positive frame of mind to make a plan of what you can do to resolve the situation that is causing you stress.

Use this exercise whenever you feel under pressure or stress. It will help you clarify your thoughts and feelings, put things into perspective, and enable you to see things in a more positive light.

Important points to remember
- Being aware of self-defeating mind-talk is the key that can open the door to challenging it.

- Self-defeating mind-talk sparks off negative feelings which lead to negative behaviour.

- Substituting mind-talk masters for mind-talk menaces can put you in a happier and more positive frame of mind.

- Always ask yourself: is this mind-talk helping me succeed?

Learning to challenge negative mind-talk and replacing it with positive mind-talk is the antidote that will enable you to become master of your own mind and destiny.

CASE STUDY 9 – FEARFUL FREDA

Freda had developed a motorway driving phobia, which was causing her stress and anxiety. This is Freda's self-help programme which she devised to overcome her phobia.

Identified reasons for phobia
1. Very near accident on slip-road going onto motorway.

2. Working for accident claims assessors and seeing photographs of appalling motorway accidents.

Goal
To be able to drive on motorways again.

Mind-talk menaces identified
- I *might* have a *dreadful* accident (*anticipating the future*).

- I *should* have been more careful (*blaming self*).

- *What if* the car goes out of control?

- I'll never be a competent driver (*predicting the future*).

Feelings identified
- Intense anxiety and fear.

Consequences of feelings
- Avoidance of motorway driving.

- Lifestyle restricted – unable to travel far alone.

- Inconvenience caused to husband, always has to drive me on any long distance journeys.

Self-help programme
1. Imagine travelling a short distance on the motorway. Practise breathing and relaxation techniques. Use positive mind-talk: 'I am a competent driver', 'motorways are not dangerous – there are far more accidents on ordinary roads'.

2. Plan a short journey – two motorway junctions. Ask husband to come with me. Choose a time when the motorway will be fairly quiet – say 8.00 am next Sunday morning. Practise breathing and relaxation techniques before going. Repeat short journeys until I feel more confident.

3. Prepare myself a homework diary to record my mind-talk and feelings, and to measure progress.

4. Plan a longer journey. Ask husband to come with me. Choose a

time when there will be slightly more traffic on the motorway – say 6.00 pm on a Saturday. Practise breathing and relaxation techniques before going.

5. Plan a short journey on my own – say three motorway junctions. Practise breathing and relaxation techniques before going.

6. Plan a longer journey on my own – to Bournemouth. Arrange to visit my friend who lives close by. Also call in a couple of superstores, and purchase something as a reward for my efforts. Take same route back home. Go out for meal in the evening to celebrate my achievement.

7. If first attempt is unsuccessful, go back to step 1 and repeat the process.

KEEPING YOUR PERSONAL DEVELOPMENT JOURNAL

It is not enough to have a good mind, the main thing is to use it well.

(René Descartes)

1. Make a note of your main mind-talk menaces. When you hear yourself saying these, say STOP to yourself quietly in your mind, and replace them with mind-talk masters.

2. Design yourself a mind-talk chart similar to the one in Figure 7. Use it to record your negative mind-talk and then challenge it with more positive mind-talk.

3. Record any negative feelings you experience, and try to identify what you were saying in your mind beforehand. Remember – feelings are generated by the messages you have been feeding your mind, so it's important to try and establish exactly what you have been saying.

4. Keep track of your negative mind-talk and ask yourself the following questions:

   • Am I predicting the future negatively?

   • Am I making things worse than they are?

	Negative mind-talk
1	
2	
3	
4	
5	
6	
7	
8	
9	
10	
11	
12	
13	
14	

	Positive mind-talk
1	
2	
3	
4	
5	
6	
7	
8	
9	
10	
11	
12	
13	
14	

Fig. 7. Example of a mind-talk chart.

- Is this mind-talk helping me succeed?
- Does it really matter if things don't turn out exactly how I want them to?

Only by making these challenges will you learn to become master of your own mind and master of your own destiny.

Correct answers to Activity 12 – Changing mind-talk menaces to mind-talk masters

Menace
I must
I can't

Master
I will
I can/won't

It's not fair	It's the way it is
It's a problem	It's a challenge
Life's a bitch	Life is what I make it
I'm useless	I'm a fallible human being
I can't cope	I feel confident I can handle it
I'm stupid	Who says so? Where's the evidence?
I should	I could
I need	I would like
It was awful	It was regrettable
Yes...but	Perhaps I could
I might	I am going to
I'm a failure	Just because I failed at... doesn't mean I'm a failure
I'm not good enough	I'm as good as the next person
I never have any luck	I make my own luck

5

Expressing Your Feelings

I wish thar was winders to my Sole, sed I, so that you could see some of my feelins.

(*The Showman's Courtship*, Artemus Ward [Charles Farrar Brown])

So far we have looked at mastering the physical symptoms of stress, and how to become masters of our own minds. But what can we do about the emotional symptoms of stress – in other words, our feelings?

What are feelings?
Feelings are our reactions to what is happening in our lives. They are as real to us as facts. It's our mind-talk that sparks our feelings, but it's our feelings that influence our behaviour. Bottled-up feelings and emotions are damaging to our psychological health and well-being. They can lead us on the path to stress and depression.

Feelings have a voice
Feelings have a voice of their own and they need to be heard. Figure 8 gives a complete picture of how Wendy (Case Study 6 in Chapter 3) gets caught in the negative stress cycle. From the case study we get a glimpse of Wendy's negative mind-talk (there's probably a lot more going on). However, even from the little bit gleaned, we can see that this is producing physical symptoms. We can also see that she is experiencing some powerful emotions, which in turn affect her behaviour.

Expressing feelings energises us and brings relief
There's nothing wrong with feelings, we all experience them, indeed expressing them energises us and brings relief. Without them we would be rather like a computer – emotionless and programmed to behave in a certain way. But problems arise when we let them fester away inside us, or we express them inappropriately, which is what happened with Wendy.

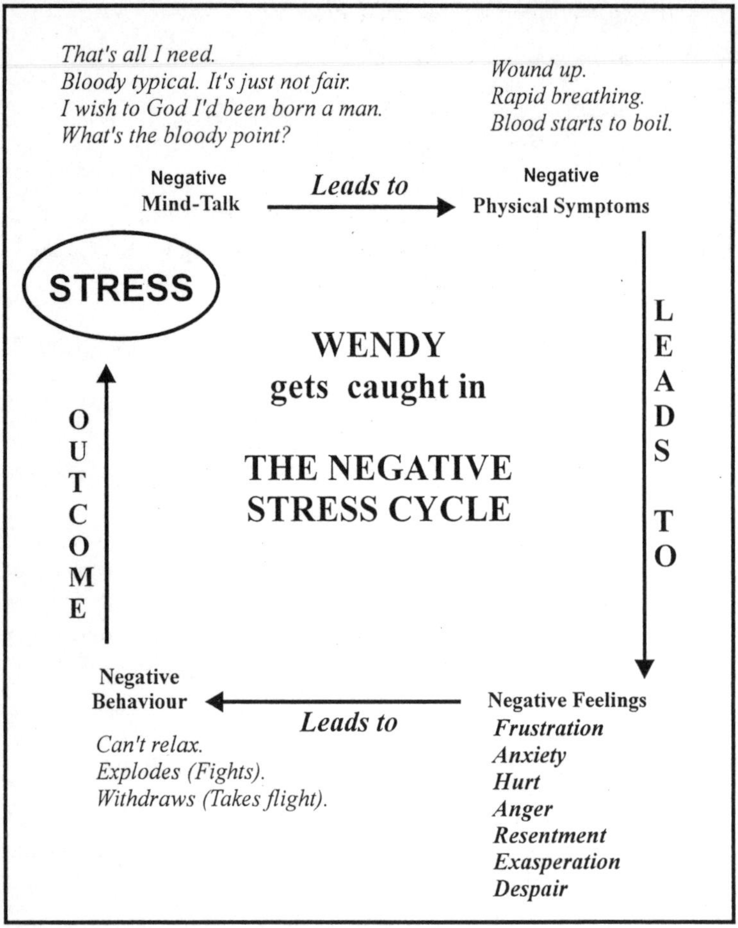

That's all I need.
Bloody typical. It's just not fair.
I wish to God I'd been born a man.
What's the bloody point?

Wound up.
Rapid breathing.
Blood starts to boil.

Negative
Mind-Talk ——— *Leads to* ———►

Negative
Physical Symptoms

(**STRESS**)

WENDY
gets caught in

THE NEGATIVE
STRESS CYCLE

O
U
T
C
O
M
E

L
E
A
D
S

T
O

Negative
Behaviour ◄——— *Leads to* ———

Can't relax.
Explodes (Fights).
Withdraws (Takes flight).

Negative Feelings
Frustration
Anxiety
Hurt
Anger
Resentment
Exasperation
Despair

Fig. 8. Wendy gets caught in the negative stress cycle.

UNDERSTANDING THE DIFFICULTIES IN EXPRESSING FEELINGS

Some people are fully in touch with their feelings and can express them assertively

These people are fortunate, they don't bottle their feelings up. They can identify exactly what they are feeling, and express their feelings honestly and assertively. They have learnt that it's acceptable to give their feelings a voice. They will says things like:

- 'I feel **really sad** about what's happened.'
- 'I feel **hurt** because you forgot our anniversary.'
- 'I feel **angry** because you have left your room in such a mess.'
- 'I feel **happy** when I am with you.'

Other people are less in touch with their feelings
These people are not quite so fortunate, although they are partially aware of their feelings. They may say things like:

- 'I'm not sure how I feel.'
- 'I feel confused.'
- 'I can't get a grip on my feelings.'
- 'I feel mixed up.'

What these people really mean is they are having difficulty sorting their feelings out. They may have learnt that it's acceptable to give their feelings a voice, but have perhaps experienced a crisis in their lives which has thrown their feelings into turmoil. However, with encouragement from a good listener, they will probably be able to identify, clarify and verbalise their true feelings.

Some people are out of touch with their feelings
These people are unfortunate. They have learnt to bottle their feelings up. They are masters at hiding or denying their feelings and may find it difficult to identify their true feelings. They will say things like:

- 'I feel numb.'
- 'I feel nothing.'
- 'I never get angry.'
- 'I have no anger in me.'
- 'I don't know how to express my feelings.'

These people have learnt that it's unacceptable to give their feelings a voice, and may well experience life as dull, boring, flat or meaningless.

Some people think they should be happy all the time and bottle up their feelings of sadness

Sadness is a natural emotion associated with loss. However, some people block off their feelings of sadness, putting a brave face on everything. Blocked sadness or grief can lead to depression. Expressed appropriately, sadness is a powerful healing agent. **Expressing sadness enables us to adjust to change**.

CONSIDERING THE EFFECTS OF CHILDHOOD CONDITIONING

Our early conditioning has a powerful influence on how we manage feelings in adult life. If we have been fortunate enough to be raised in a family where the expression of feelings, both positive and negative, was encouraged, we learn that sharing feelings is normal, acceptable, healthy.

Unfortunately, the reverse is also true. If we were raised in a family where expressing feelings was actively discouraged, we learn to hide or deny them. We may grow up believing that if we show our feelings other people will manipulate us, or that it's 'soft' to express emotions. If we were raised in a family where only negative feelings were expressed we may only be aware of negative feelings. If we were raised in a hostile atmosphere where only anger, aggression or violence was expressed, we may grow up believing that anger, aggression and violence are normal and acceptable behaviour.

Understanding the effects of our childhood blueprint

What we hear and see is what we learn. As children, we do not think to question or challenge our parents' beliefs because we perceive our parents as 'all knowing and powerful' – the people who know what's best for us. Think back to your early childhood and reflect for a few minutes on the statements below. Do any of them sound familiar?

- It upsets me to see you crying like that.

- Be brave.

- Be strong.

- Don't be such a cry baby.

- Big boys don't cry.

- Don't be such a big girl's blouse.

- Pull yourself together.
- Get a grip of yourself.
- Anger is bad.
- Don't you dare show aggression in this house.
- Just wait 'til your Dad gets home.
- I'll get my belt to you if you don't stop that whinging.

Messages like these are internalised by a child and interpreted in her own language. They become the child's blueprint for living – her pattern of behaviour. To demonstrate how this works in practice, let us imagine a young child regularly hearing messages similar to those above. How might she interpret these in her own language? Figure 9 gives an example.

I must not cry. Crying is a sign of weakness.

↓

I must always be strong and in control.

↓

I must not show my feelings.

↓

I must not get angry – anger is bad.

↓

**I must not let Mummy see that I am upset,
because she might get upset too.**

Fig. 9. An example of one child's blueprint for living.

Considering your own childhood blueprint
Think about your own blueprint for living. Are you carrying around any childhood messages that get in the way of you expressing your feelings in adult life?

WITNESSING THE EFFECTS OF SWALLOWING FEELINGS

Not giving a voice to our feelings, particularly negative feelings, can cause havoc to our psychological and physical well-being. Feelings do not go away. They fester away inside us just waiting to find an escape route. Unexpressed negative feelings have a nasty habit of manifesting themselves in disguised form.

CASE STUDY 10 – ANGRY ALICE

Alice was recovering from a severe migraine. On the day it started her son had telephoned to say he was spending the weekend with his Dad, and to seek her approval. Alice's initial feeling was one of **shock**, because her son had not seen his father for seven years (since Alice and her son's father had divorced). In addition to feeling shocked, Alice felt **hurt**. However, both feelings were swallowed down. She responded: 'Of course I don't mind you spending the weekend with your Dad.' This was a lie, because she minded a lot – she felt **betrayed**. She then felt **guilty** and **selfish** for feeling this way, which added to her distress. To anaesthetise her emotional pain she swallowed these unacceptable feelings down too, but they didn't go away. They found their escape route in the form of a physical ailment – a migraine.

Alice gets in touch with her feelings

Alice's friend called by to see how she was, and she talked to her friend about the situation. Her face got redder and redder as her feelings started flooding to the surface. She was surprised to discover that underlying the feelings of shock, hurt, betrayal, guilt, and selfishness, another very powerful emotion was lurking – **anger**. This took Alice completely aback, because anger was an unfamiliar and uncomfortable feeling for her – *expressing anger had been taboo in her family.*

However, with encouragement from her friend, Alice vented her wrath about the situation. When she had finished verbalising her anger, she breathed a huge sigh of relief. After her friend had gone, she noticed that the tail end of her migraine had disappeared completely, and she felt a lot lighter.

TAKING THE RISK OF EXPRESSING FEELINGS

If we have not been used to giving our feelings a voice, the very thought of verbalising our emotions can seem very risky. We may be full of *what ifs* . . .

- '*What if* I hurt him or her?'
- '*What if* he or she rejects me?'
- '*What if* he or she takes offence?'
- '*What if* it makes the situation worse?'

- '*What if* he or she gets angry with me?'

Or we may:

- *fear* being exposed

- *fear* losing face if we show our feelings.

All too often, therefore, we minimise the risk by swallowing our feelings and putting on a brave face.

The pros of expressing feelings

- It relieves pressure and tension.

- It is therapeutic.

- When feelings are brought out into the open there is more chance that something constructive can be done with them.

- Feelings have a voice of their own and we need to let them speak for themselves.

- Expressing feelings energises us.

- Expressing feelings openly and honestly can positively enhance our physical and psychological well-being.

- Expressing feelings encourages closeness and intimacy, and reduces misunderstandings. (*Remember, other people are not mind readers, they can only be guided by what we tell them.*)

- Expressing feelings increases self-awareness and enables other people to get to know us better.

- Expressing feelings gives permission to other people to express theirs.

The cons of bottling feelings up

- Repressing feelings depletes our energy.

- Hiding or denying our feelings can severely affect our psychological and physical well-being, which can lead to stress-related illness.

- It is now well documented that bottled-up anger, or anger turned in on ourselves, can lead to stress and depression. Unexpressed hate, guilt, shame, bitterness and resentment can also take a considerable toll on our bodies and minds.

So, although expressing feelings may seem risky, there can be a much higher price to pay for bottling them up.

MODIFYING OUR CHILDHOOD BLUEPRINT

Changing established behaviour patterns is not easy because it involves taking risks, and the risk factor can seem incredibly scary to begin with. As behaviour is influenced by feelings, to change behaviour we need to start becoming more aware of our feelings.

Listening to our body
Our body is the most reliable source of information for identifying feelings. For example:

- If we experience a warm, glowing or 'jelly like' sensation this could indicate we are happy or excited.

- If we experience a 'knotted up' or 'churned up' sensation this could be symptomatic of stress or anxiety.

- If we experience a sinking sensation this could imply we are depressed or despondent.

- If we experience a lump in our throat this could point to feeling sad.

- If the hairs on the back of our neck seem to be standing on end this could signify fear and terror.

- If our inside feels like it's about to explode this could suggest anger or rage.

Watching for non-verbal clues
> Words may be false and full of art,
> Sighs are the natural language of the heart.
>> (Thomas Shadwell)

Feelings also have a tendency to escape via our body language – we 'act out' our emotional state through our gestures, posture and voice tone. Monitoring our body language can therefore provide us with further valuable clues to identifying our feelings. For example:

- If we feel happy we will smile, laugh, be jolly. Our body will feel relaxed, our gestures open and expressive. Our tone of voice will be enthusiastic.

- If we feel angry we will glare, scowl or grit our teeth. We may wag a finger, clench our fists, or impatiently tap our fingers on the arms of a chair or table. Our body will feel rigid. Our tone of voice will be harsh or loud.

- If we feel sad we may force a smile, our mouth might quiver, we may sigh, shrug our shoulders or bury our head in our hands. Our body will feel heavy. Our voice may be barely audible.

- If we feel stressed, anxious or nervous we may erect barriers to protect ourselves. We will try to shut the 'enemy' out by crossing our legs and arms. We may fidget, twiddle with a strand of hair or item of jewellery, wring our hands or bite our nails. Our body will feel tense or shaky. Our tone of voice will probably be meek.

It is estimated that between 60 and 80 per cent of our communication is transmitted non-verbally. Therefore by gaining insight into your own body language you will have acquired a powerful tool for understanding yourself better. This increased self-knowledge will also give you greater insight into how other people 'act out' their emotional state via their body language. Close observation of other people's body language can be fascinating and very revealing.

Over the next week, without making it blatantly obvious, make a conscious effort to watch your family, friends, work colleagues or boss, and see whether you can decode how they might be feeling from their body messages. However, do bear in mind that no matter how skilled we think we might be at reading body language we can still misinterpret the signals sometimes!

FINDING THE RIGHT WORDS TO DESCRIBE THE FEELING

We all experience a wide range of feelings and emotions, but if we have been discouraged from expressing them, we may have a limited vocabulary of words to describe our feelings accurately.

ACTIVITY 15 – Increasing your awareness of feeling words

Read through the following list of feeling words and place a tick alongside any that sound familiar to you.

absorbed
accepted
affectionate
afraid
aimless
amazed
amused
angry
anguished
antagonistic
anxious
appreciated
apprehensive
ashamed
awkward
bad
bitter
blue
bored
broken-hearted
buoyant
calm
carefree
caring
certain
cheerful
comfortable
confident
confused
contented
cool
creative
defiant
delighted
depressed
desperate
determined
devastated
disappointed
discouraged
disgusted
dislike
dismay
distressed
disturbed
doubtful
dubious

eager
elated
embarrassed
empty
encouraged
energetic
enjoyed
enthusiastic
envious
exasperated
excited
exhausted
exhilarated
fascinated
fearful
fragile
fragmented
free
frustrated
furious
futile
gloomy
glum
grateful
grief
grumpy
guilty
happy
hateful
helpful
helpless
hopeful
hopeless
horrified
hostile
hurt
impatient
inadequate
inferior
insecure
interested
involved
isolated
jealous
joyful
lazy
let down

lonely
lost
loving
mean
miserable
motivated
moved
numb
optimistic
overjoyed
overwhelmed
passionate
peaceful
powerful
proud
quiet
rage
rejected
relaxed
relieved
resentful
sad
satisfied
secure
sensitive
shocked
silly
sorry
stifled
stimulated
suspicious
tense
terrified
threatened
tormented
trapped
uncomfortable
uneasy
unhappy
upset
useless
valued
victimised
vulnerable
worried
worthless

How many have you ticked? Are you surprised at the wide range of feelings you experience? Now mark those you see as negative feelings with an asterisk and record them in your journal under the heading 'Feelings I experience as negative'.

UNDERSTANDING LEVELS OF FEELINGS

There are many words to describe the same feeling, and each individual has their own unique feeling language. Whereas the words I choose to describe my feelings might feel acceptable to me, they might feel totally alien to you. For example, I might say 'I feel absolutely furious with you for...', whereas you might say 'I feel cross with you for...'. It's possible we both mean the same thing, but we are expressing our feeling on a level that feels comfortable to us. Perhaps underlying your feeling of 'I feel cross' is a more powerful emotion such as rage or fury which feels more risky to admit.

Expressing your feelings accurately involves being honest about how you feel. Being honest about how you feel necessitates getting in touch with your level of feelings. Recognising the depth of your feelings by listening carefully to what your body is telling you is the most reliable way of checking out whether you are being honest – and remember, **feelings rarely lie**.

ACTIVITY 16 – Expanding awareness of feelings

Joy, anger, fear and sadness are four basic feelings we all experience. To expand your awareness of the many different words people use to describe these feelings select the word *joy*, and fill the outer circle (see Figure 10) with alternative words to describe joy. Repeat the same process with the remaining three feelings. Try to find at least ten alternative words for each feeling. When you have finished, compare your alternative words with those provided at the end of the chapter. Then consider which feeling words you identify with most.

PUTTING YOUR FEELINGS INTO WORDS

Once you have identified exactly what you are feeling, the next stage is to communicate those feelings honestly. This involves:

● Owning your feelings (*this is how I feel*).

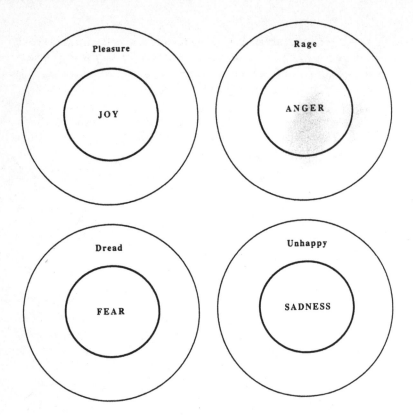

Fig. 10. Expanding awareness of feelings.

- Taking responsibility for your feelings (*I'm entitled to my feelings*).

Owning and taking responsibility for feelings avoids blaming other people.

This may be a difficult concept to grasp immediately because very often we believe that other people are responsible for how we feel. However, this is simply not true. Think about it. Does anyone hold a gun to your head insisting that you feel hurt, sad, enraged or depressed? Circumstances may influence our feelings, but nobody makes us feel anything – we do this all by ourselves. Blaming someone else for how we feel is counter-productive because it tends to put the other person in a position where they feel a need to defend themselves from our attack. For example, how would you feel if I said to you: 'You've upset me' or 'You've made me very angry'? You might defend your position by responding with: 'You blame me for everything' or 'You're always getting on your high horse about something'. This could add fuel to the already burning embers, and lead me to defend my position with a counter-attack such as: 'You don't give a damn about my feelings' or 'You just don't understand how I feel'. Needless to say this type of communication is hardly conducive to a harmonious relationship.

Owning feelings, and taking responsibility for them, involves communicating both positive and negative feelings openly and honestly.

USING AN ASSERTIVE APPROACH TO EXPRESS YOUR FEELINGS

The following assertive approach is a productive way to express feelings:

- 'I feel... (*describe emotion*) with you because... (*give reason*).'

- 'I feel... (*describe emotion*) about ... (*give reason*).'

Adopting this approach enables you to express your feelings and the reason for your feelings. It is honest and clear communication. By using 'I' statements you are taking responsibility. You are not blaming the other person. To get out of the blaming trap you need to eliminate unassertive statements from your vocabulary.

Examples of unassertive statements
- 'You have made me... (*describe emotion – no reason*).'
  For example: '*You've made me very upset.*'

- 'You have ... (*describe emotion*) me (*no reason*).'
  For example: 'You've hurt me.'

Example of assertive statements
- 'I *love* being with you.'

- 'I *really appreciate* it when you help me with the housework.'

- 'I am feeling *very apprehensive* about this interview.'
- 'I feel *annoyed* because you have broken your promise.'
- 'I feel *angry* with you for leaving the kitchen in such a mess.'
- 'I feel *uneasy* about this forthcoming exam.'
- 'I feel *confused* about the situation.'
- 'I feel *anxious* about flying.'
- 'I feel *hopeful* that things will improve.'
- 'I feel *exhausted.*'
- 'I feel *embarrassed* when I stammer.'

Avoiding indirect statements

Using the words 'one' or 'we' are indirect ways of expressing feelings. For example:

- 'One doesn't do things like that.'
- 'We feel this course is a load of rubbish.'

In the first example, what the person really means is: '**I** wouldn't do it like that', or '**I** don't approve'. In the second, what the person really means is: '**I** feel this course is a load of rubbish'. By using the 'we', which is a generalisation (*no two people ever feel exactly the same*), this person is taking the safe option.

ACTIVITY 17 – Owning and taking responsibility for your feelings

This next activity is designed to help you practise owning and taking responsibility for your feelings. If it feels appropriate, add the word **you** after the statement. For example, I feel happy when **you**...

I feel... when	Complete the statements
I feel happy when	_____
I feel angry when	_____
I feel frightened when	_____
I feel sad when	_____

I feel stimulated when _____

I feel anxious when _____

I feel envious when _____

I feel jealous when _____

I feel furious when _____

I feel scared when _____

I feel depressed when _____

I feel motivated when _____

I feel hurt when _____

I feel relaxed when _____

I feel vulnerable when _____

I feel confident when _____

I feel intimidated when _____

I feel ashamed when _____

I feel guilty when _____

I feel proud when _____

I feel useful when _____

PUTTING YOUR LEARNING INTO PRACTICE

I hear and I forget, I see and I remember, I do and I understand.

(Chinese proverb)

By now you will hopefully have established a clearer picture of your feelings, and identified situations which give rise to those feelings. This is valuable learning. However, it's one thing knowing, it's another putting that learning into practice. The only way to become proficient at any new skill is by testing it out – **by doing**. Look back over your responses to the previous activity. Are there any statements on your list you could risk sharing with the person concerned? If you feel sufficiently confident **do it**, then monitor the response you get. If you still feel hesitant, role-play your statements with someone you trust. Ask the person for feedback. For example:

- 'Did what I've just said come across assertively?'

- 'How did what I've just said sound to you?'

Remember, it takes practice to gain self-confidence.

MANAGING ANGER AND FEAR

The focus of the remainder of this chapter is on anger and fear, as these are the two main emotions aroused in us when we feel threatened. Anger equips us with energy to confront the threat (*fight*), and fear provides us with energy to flee from the threat (*take flight*). Yet, as we saw demonstrated in the four situations at the beginning of Chapter 1, if the root cause of the anger or fear is not dealt with appropriately, or is avoided, energy released at the 'threatening stage' can remain bottled up instead of getting used up.

Refer to your journal

Have you included anger and fear on your list of negative feelings? You may well have recorded other feelings such as jealous, envious, guilty, bitter, depressed, resentful. These feelings can also generate stress. However, it would be impossible to do justice to these emotions within the space of one chapter. Listed in the further reading section is a range of books which specifically address some of these difficult emotions, and you may well want to put these on your future reading list. Included in this list, too, are books entirely devoted to the subjects of fear and anger, which you might well want to read to gain increased awareness. Susan Jeffers' book, *Feel the Fear and Do It Anyway*, is an excellent self-help book on how to overcome fear and increase your self-confidence.

DEALING WITH ANGER CONSTRUCTIVELY

Anger channelled appropriately can help us solve our problems. However, if a much bottled-up anger explodes inappropriately it can result in aggression or violence. Reflect on the following quote from a poem by William Blake:

> I was angry with my friend:
> I told my wrath my wrath did end.
> I was angry with my foe:
> I told it not, my wrath did grow.

How would you interpret his words in your own language? In the box below is my interpretation, from which you will see I have used each letter of the word ANGER to emphasise the points which I believe he was making, *ie*:

1. expressing anger brings relief

2. bottling up anger brings us grief.

Air → **Negative** → **Grievances** → **Experience** → **Relief**

ANGER

Avoid → **Negative** → **Grievances** → **Expect** → **Repercussions**

Why do we get angry?

As mentioned earlier, we get angry when we feel threatened. We can also get angry if things don't go our way. We feel hurt, wounded, upset, or that it's dreadful not to get what we want. Children stamp their feet, sulk, or throw a tantrum if they don't get their own way. Do we behave any differently as adults? I think not. We might use slightly different tactics, but they all amount to the same childlike behaviour. We rant and rave, seethe in silence to punish the person we are angry with, or bully other people until they give in to our demands. Nobody makes us angry – we make it happen all by ourselves. So, if this is the case, we also have the ability to calm ourselves down.

Misplaced anger

Think about how often you have taken your anger out on the wrong person. For example, have you felt angry with your boss, but bitten your lip for fear of losing your job, and then come home and taken it out on your partner or kids?

RECOGNISING THE PRICE OF UNLEASHING UNCONTROLLED ANGER

Anger supplies the arms.

(Virgil)

The consequences of letting go of uncontrolled anger can have devastating and far-reaching effects.

Example

Steven served as a juror on a murder trial, where a man was sentenced to life imprisonment for killing another man. You may be thinking to yourself that the man deserved everything he got. Steven did not condone this man's actions. However, he did feel an element of great sadness at the total devastation caused by this man's inability to control his anger. The cost in this case was a man's life, a family grieving over the loss of their son, the defendant incarcerated, his wife left to bring up three children alone, and the taxpayer picking up the tab.

> If we hate a person, we hate something in our image of him that lies within ourselves. What is not within ourselves doesn't upset us.
>
> (Hermann Hesse)

Letting go of anger

Anger stored in the body needs physical or emotional release. We need to:

1. Acknowledge that we are feeling angry.

2. Analyse it – *why am I feeling angry?*

3. Express it – *by finding an appropriate way of getting the anger out.*

GIVING YOURSELF PERMISSION TO BE ANGRY

Some people consider they have no right to be angry. Are you one of these people? Donna was. When she was asked to design herself an anger rights charter on an assertiveness course she looked aghast. At the end of the session her sheet of paper was still blank, although she had watched and listened attentively as the other students prepared their charters. However, when Donna arrived at the next session she looked as pleased as punch. She had discovered to her amazement that she felt she did have some rights after all, and had prepared her charter at home (see Figure 11). What was even more significant was that she'd taken the risk of expressing two of the rights she'd allowed herself to have, which had proved a very productive and liberating experience for her.

Reviewing Donna's anger rights charter

Read through Donna's anger rights charter and then consider your own beliefs about anger. You will note that Donna has used 'I' statements, thus taking responsibility for her anger, and has also included other strategies for dealing with anger. This is very important, because ill-timed expression of anger can do more damage than good. For example, getting angry at someone in the middle of a wedding or funeral service is hardly likely to make you flavour of the month. It could also prove a humiliating or belittling experience for the person on the receiving end. Another reason why it's important to include other strategies is because your anger may be aimed at someone who is no longer around, so you cannot express it directly.

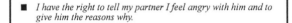

■ *I have the right to tell my partner I feel angry with him and to give him the reasons why.*

■ *I have the right to tell my friend I am angry with her when she keeps me waiting.*

■ *I have the right to feel angry when I keep being interrupted.*

■ *I have the right to protect myself from other people's anger.*

■ *I have the right to feel angry when I am not being listened to.*

■ *I have the right to feel angry when I know I am being lied to.*

■ *I have the right to feel angry when I am not treated with respect.*

■ *I have the right to feel angry when my privacy is invaded.*

Other constructive strategies for dealing with my anger

- I can choose not to share my anger if I think it will be detrimental to me. I can save it for a more appropriate time.
- I can talk my angry feelings through with my friend.
- I can vent my anger by writing it down or by drawing it.
- I can physically release my anger by going for a long walk, thumping a pillow, digging the garden, doing some vigorous exercise, tearing up some old telephone directories.

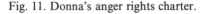

Fig. 11. Donna's anger rights charter.

ACTIVITY 18 – Designing your own anger rights charter

When you feel ready, design your own anger rights charter. Remember to use 'I statements', and don't forget to include other strategies for releasing your anger. When you have finished, put your anger rights charter in a prominent place to remind yourself of the rights you have given yourself permission to have.

ACTIVITY 19 – Writing your anger out

Writing can be a very therapeutic way of releasing bottled-up anger, and is particularly useful if you cannot confront the person directly; for example, if the person is no longer around, or has died.

Who are you angry with?

Reflect on anyone from the past who you still feel angry with. Make a list of their names. Rank them in order of how angry you feel. For example, if you have written down five names, make number one the person you feel most angry with and number five the person you feel least angry with. Working through your list in reverse order, write a letter to each person telling them exactly what they did that hurt you and why you still feel angry with them. If it helps, draw pictures or symbols – anything that enables you to get the angry feelings out of your body.

Forgiveness is the key to freedom

A man that studieth revenge keeps his own wounds green.

(Francis Bacon)

When you have finished each letter, think about whether you can forgive the person. This may prove extremely difficult. However, hate, bitterness, revenge and resentment can wreak havoc to our bodies and minds, so you are not doing yourself any favours by hanging on to these painful feelings. **You are the one who's hurting you** – is that what you really want or deserve? **The past cannot be changed, but the future can**, and it's worth remembering this. If you feel able to, tell the person at the end of your letter that you have forgiven them.

A word of warning

This can be a powerful exercise and it may leave you feeling emotionally drained after you have released your feelings. However, you have got the feelings out of your body which is the most important thing, and within a short space of time you will probably experience a feeling of lightness and relief. Allow yourself plenty of time between writing your letters, and give yourself a reward for having the courage and strength to face your feelings.

CASE STUDY 11 – COURAGEOUS CAROL

Carol decided to write a letter to her deceased father. This is what she wrote.

Dear Dad,
I loved you so much, and I know you loved me, but it seems such a shame that we were never able to tell each other. I understand why now, and somehow that eases the pain just a little, yet it still hurts that you died without hearing me say how much I cared about you.

I can remember, as if it was yesterday, sitting at your bedside holding your hand, praying that you would get better. I felt so helpless and inadequate. There was so much I wanted to say, but I couldn't find the words, and you were too sick to listen.

There were times after you died Dad when I felt consumed with anger. I felt angry with you for leaving me, and then guilty because I felt angry. Some of this anger was triggered by childhood memories; the times when I felt lost and alone, and longed for you to be there to cuddle and reassure me. And the times when I needed your support and encouragement, but you were always too busy to notice, or were not at home. I know now that you had your reasons, but it hurts all the same.

Often Dad, I think about you, and Christmas has never felt quite the same since you died. Gone is the laughter, the singing, the music; all those happy and precious moments we shared together. Yet, they are indelibly printed in my mind, hold a very special place in my heart, and it comforts me to know that nobody can take those joyous memories away.

I know I cannot bring you back Dad, but when I feel a need to bring you closer, I read a poem which I wrote about you shortly after you died. It still brings tears to my eyes, mixed tears of sadness and happiness. I would like to share my poem with you now Dad.

I watched you slowly dying, drugged and in great pain,
I held your hand feeling utterly helpless;
consciousness you didn't regain.
I felt the tears well up inside; your pain gone, you'd passed away,
and a part of me went with you on that January day.
You'd given up your will to live, which made me so terribly sad.
Because you were my special friend, the man I loved,
you were a very precious Dad.

I feel sad about not having the courage to tell you how special you were to me when you were alive and healthy, and can only console myself with the thought that in the closeness we shared you probably knew anyway.

Dad, I forgive you for the times when you weren't there for me. I'm sure you were oblivious to the pain it caused me, and I didn't tell you. I hope, wherever you are, that you are happy and at peace.

Goodbye, and God Bless.

I love you Dad.

Carol.

IDENTIFYING OTHER CONSTRUCTIVE STRATEGIES FOR DEALING WITH ANGER

When angry count four; when very angry swear.

(Mark Twain)

- Do some vigorous exercise, or go for a long walk.

- Throw some old crockery or glasses against a wall. However, be sure there is no one around to get hurt.

- Take a trip to the country, or to another private place where you can scream, shout, rant and rave, without being heard.

- Buy yourself a punch-bag.

- Thump a cushion or pillow.

- Twist a towel, or something similar, and beat it against a wall.

- With a trusted friend, role-play the situation that is making you angry, and say what you want to say.

- Walk away from the situation if you feel yourself getting

incensed, calm yourself down, and share your feelings later when you have regained your composure.

- Count to ten under your breath before saying anything. This may give you sufficient time to calm down, and prevent you putting your foot in it.

- Show respect for the other person (remember, they have feelings too). Listen to what the other person has to say, and ask questions to clarify the real issue.

- Work towards win-win situations and be prepared to compromise.

- If you are faced with another's wrath, and it feels appropriate, try using light-hearted humour to defuse the situation. Remain as calm as you can. It's very hard for another person to stay angry for long if he or she is met with someone who keeps their cool.

- Try the empty chair technique. Place two chairs facing each other and pretend the person you are angry with is sitting facing you. *Express how you feel to that person.*

Counselling for anger

If you are carrying around a lot of unresolved anger, or are expressing it inappropriately, working things through with a counsellor may be the key to understanding what lies at the root of your anger. It can also provide you with the opportunity to explore and develop more constructive strategies for managing it.

Examples of inappropriate expressions of anger

- lashing out at the wrong people/exploding for no apparent reason
- bullying others
- self-destructive behaviour, *eg*;
  - suppressing anger by stuffing down food, abusing alcohol or drugs
  - overworking
  - self-harming
- turning it in on yourself (which can lead to stress and depression).

Some important points to remember about anger

The man who gets angry at the right things and with the right people, and in the right way and at the right time, and for the right length of time, is commended.

(Aristotle)

1. *Nobody makes us angry*. We do it all by ourselves. We are responsible for it, and we have the power within us to calm ourselves down.

2. *Anger is a natural emotion*. Provided it is channelled appropriately, it helps us solve our problems.

3. *Bottled-up anger is dangerous*. Unleashed aggression in the form of violence or hurling verbal abuse is totally unacceptable and destructive. Words are lethal when they are used as a weapon. They should be used with care and sensitivity. We can build our relationships by using the right words, but we can destroy our relationships by choosing the wrong ones. **We can never take words back**.

4. Suppressed aggression becomes depression.

CONQUERING FEAR

No passion so effectually robs the mind of all its powers of acting and reasoning as fear.

(Edmund Burke)

Nobody goes through life without any fears, because living itself is a risky business, and taking risks generates fear. None of us knows what's around the corner, or what the future holds in store for us. Sometimes life runs smoothly; at other times we can be faced with major difficulties to overcome. Life is a bit like a lottery – the difference being that with life we only get one bite at the cherry. There are no guarantees – if we get it wrong we can't send it back and ask for a replacement, and nobody offers us an extended warranty against faulty components!

How life's going to be is down to me
It's up to us to ensure we get the best out of life, even when the odds seem heavily stacked against us. We are the ones who ultimately have to choose how we lead our lives. On the one hand, we might be the type of person who decides that running away from our fears is the easiest and safest option. On the other hand, we might be the

type of person who chooses to fight through the fear barrier. Whichever choice we make influences our lives. By running away from our fears we risk the chance of stress, and may experience life as boring or unrewarding – which we might bitterly regret at some stage. By fighting our fears we increase our chance of experiencing life as rewarding, we give ourselves the opportunity to maximise our full potential and we gain self-confidence in the process. So isn't fighting fear worth the gamble?

Basically, when we feel frightened, we are saying to ourselves something like 'I couldn't possibly do that – it's too risky!' So it's back to negative mind-talk again, which we constantly need to challenge if we are determined to conquer our fears. There are also some other very useful techniques which we can add to our repertoire of skills. See Figure 12 – the fighting fear formula.

CASE STUDY 12 – STAMMERING STAN

Using the fighting fear formula.

Situation
Stan was a student on an assertiveness course. He was asked by the trainer to give a presentation to the other students on the benefits of assertive communication.

Stage 1 – Facing the fear
Stan's first step was to admit to his wife that he was frightened about doing the presentation because of his stammer (*a trouble shared is a trouble halved*).

Stage 2 – Exploring the fear
Stan asked himself:

1. Why am I so afraid?
    Answers: 'I am afraid people will ridicule me.'
              'I am afraid of making a fool of myself.'

2. What is the worst thing that could possibly happen?
    Answer: 'The students will go to sleep or walk out.'

3. What choices have I got?
    Answers: 'I could leave the course.'
              'I could go sick on the night.'

Facing the Fear

This stage involves acknowledging that you are frightened.

Exploring the Fear

This stage involves asking yourself some questions:
Why am I so afraid?
What is the worst thing that could possibly happen?
What choices have I got?

Assessing the Risk

This stage involves:
Examining negative mind-talk.
Assessing your level of feelings on a scale of 1 - 3.
Challenging negative mind-talk.
Re-assessing your level of feelings on a scale of 1 - 3.

Reducing the Risk

This stage involves asking yourself some more questions:
Can I handle this on my own?
Do I need support?
Who can give me that support?
What steps can I take to reduce the risk?
&
Re-assessing your level of feelings on a scale of 1 - 3.
Developing a strategy for reviewing your progress.
&

Reaping the **R**eward *for your courage and hard work.*

Fig. 12. The fighting fear formula.

'I could talk to the trainer and share my anxieties.'
'I could do it and face the consequences.'

Stage 3 – Assessing the risk

Examining negative mind-talk
This is what Stan was saying to himself:

- 'I might seize up and that would be disastrous.'

- 'I know they will laugh at me and that will make me stammer even more.'

- 'I hate standing up and speaking in front of a group of people.'

- 'What if I'm put on the spot, and can't answer their questions?'

Assessing level of feelings
These are the feelings Stan identified as a result of his negative mind-talk:

- Anxiety, dread, panic, petrified.
  Assessed on a scale of 1–3. (Stan rated his feelings as 3 – intense.)
  1.   Mild   2.   Moderate   3.   Intense.

Challenging negative mind-talk
Stan challenged his negative mind-talk with:

- 'If I do seize up it won't be the end of the world.'

- 'They already know I stammer, and nobody has laughed at me yet.'

- 'It won't be easy standing up in front of the group. However, if I could do it, it would be a great accomplishment.'

- 'They know I'm not an expert, and won't expect me to have all the answers.'

Re-assessing level of feelings
These are the feelings Stan identified as a result of challenging his mind-talk:

- Apprehensive, less anxious, uneasy, nervous.
  Assessed on a scale of 1–3. (Stan rated his feelings as 2 – moderate.)

Stage 4 – Reducing the Risk
Stan asked himself:

1. Can I handle this on my own?
   Answer: 'Yes, if I prepare my presentation well.'

2. Do I need support?
   Answer: 'Yes.'

3. Who can give me that support?
   Answers: 'My wife.' 'The students.' 'Myself.'

4. What steps can I take to reduce the risk?
   Answer: 'I will make a detailed plan.'

Stan then went on to write his plan as follows:

- I will do my homework thoroughly so I'll be well prepared on the night.

- I'll run through my presentation with my wife and ask her for feedback on ways to improve it.

- I'll do a video rehearsal to see how it comes across.

- I'll admit to the students right at the start how nervous I am because of my stammer, and ask them to bear with me.

- I'll use some humour, for example:
  'If you do notice a pr-pr-pr-pregnant pause, please feel free to chat amongst yourselves, or stretch your legs. Normal service will be resumed as soon as pur-pur-pur-possible.'
  'It might take me twice as long to give my presentation as it would for you more fluent speakers, but you'll get value for money as something *repeated* se-se-se-several times tends to sink in more.'

- I could focus my presentation on how stammerers could be helped by learning to communicate more assertively.

Re-assessing level of feelings
These are the feelings Stan identified as a result of preparing his detailed plan:

- Apprehensive, nervous, excited, enthusiastic.
  Assessed on a scale of 1–3. (Stan rated his feelings as 1 – mild.)

Developing a strategy for reviewing progress
Stan decided that his strategy for reviewing progress would be to:

- Check out with the students how his presentation came across by inviting feedback; for example, was it too long/short? Was there anything else they would have liked included?

Stan's big day arrived

He still felt nervous, which even the most experienced speakers do before giving a speech. However, this extra rush of adrenalin was just what the doctor ordered, because it motivated him to give of his best. There was no ridicule, no students going to sleep or talking amongst themselves. In fact, Stan received a standing ovation for his presentation. When he got home that evening he once more re-assessed his feelings, which produced a very different picture.

- **He felt proud and elated.**
- **Stan Fought his Fear and Reaped the Reward.**

When Stan had finished the assertiveness course, he set up a group to help other stammerers overcome their fears of public speaking. It proved an overwhelming success.

We can see from Stan's story how following the stages of the fighting fear formula, together with thoughtful planning, helped him conquer his fear.

KEEPING YOUR PERSONAL DEVELOPMENT JOURNAL

Fear has many eyes and can see things underground.
(Miguel de Cervantes)

1. Reflect on how feelings were managed in your family of origin, and then write a brief summary of how you manage you feelings in adult life. Compare whether there are any links.

2. Make a list of your top five fears. Assess the level of fear associated with each on a scale of:

   1. Mild   2. Moderate   3. Intense.

   Using your mind's eye imagine how differently your life would be if you conquered these fears.

3. Identify a situation you feel angry about. Write a description of the situation. Record what steps you could take that would help you unbottle this anger.

Revenge is a dish that tastes better cold.

(Proverb)

ACTIVITY 16 – Expanding awareness of feelings
Alternative feeling words for the four basic feelings

Joy	*Anger*	*Fear*	*Sad*
Delighted	Furious	Terrified	Blue
Blissful	Seething	Anxious	Cheerless
Ecstatic	Resentful	Horrified	Depressed
Elated	Indignant	Apprehensive	Gloomy
Jubilant	Irate	Agitated	Melancholy
Cheerful	Exasperated	Scared	Sorrowful
Happy	Riled	Petrified	Dejected
Jolly	Incensed	Dismayed	Mournful
Rapturous	Annoyed	Dread	Low-spirited
Gleeful	Irritable	Alarmed	Down

6

Communicating Skilfully

Words are, of course, the most powerful drug used by mankind.

(Rudyard Kipling)

Mastering the art of skilful communication brings many rewards, which can take us further along the path towards thriving on stress. Why? Because effective communication helps us feel nourished and deeply satisfied, rather like we do when we've just eaten a delicious meal. Lack of effective communication, on the other hand, can leave us feeling undernourished, impoverished and in need, which can be a recipe for stress.

IDENTIFYING THE SPECIFIC ADVANTAGES OF COMMUNICATING SKILFULLY

- It helps other people know who we truly are.

- It helps other people understand why we do what we do.

- It enriches our relationships.

- It reduces misunderstandings and helps us manage conflict situations.

- It improves our chances of getting our needs met.

- It encourages other people to express their needs more openly and honestly.

- It increases self-confidence and builds self-esteem (see also Chapter 7, which is dedicated to this subject).

- It helps us to feel more positively about ourselves and our lives.

PINPOINTING THE DISADVANTAGES OF POOR COMMUNICATION

- It can cause problems in our relationships. It is often at the root of relationship breakdowns.

- It causes confusion.

- It causes conflict and misunderstandings.

- It reduces our chances of getting our needs met.

- It causes frustration and resentment.

In Chapter 5 you became acquainted with two key components of skilful communication – using an assertive approach to express feelings and observing body language. The aim of this chapter is to familiarise you with the essential qualities and additional skills that can help you develop more fruitful communication.

UNDERSTANDING HOW WE COMMUNICATE

Each one of us has our own unique style of communicating. We do it automatically without giving much consideration to how it comes across to other people. Figure 13 shows a variety of communication styles together with their effect.

I must indeed, try hard to control the talking habit, but I'm afraid that little can be done, as my case is hereditary. My mother, too, is fond of chatting, and has handed this weakness down to me.

(Anne Frank)

ACTIVITY 20 – Recognising the styles of communication

1. Which style(s) do you recognise in yourself? You may see more than one.

2. Think about people you communicate with regularly, *eg* family members, friends, your boss, your work colleagues. Which styles do you recognise in them?

	Style	Effect
The aggressor	Humiliates other people. Puts people down.	*Violates other people's air space.*
The artful dodger	Listens – but never gives anything away (secretive).	*Avoids contributing to the air space.*
The asserter	Expresses self clearly and honestly. Listens to others.	*Respects other people's air space.*
The babbler	Flits about – goes off at a tangent (confuses the issue).	*Clogs up the air space.*
The bombarder	Talks but never listens.	*Hogs the air space.*
The bragger	Been there – done it – got the T-shirt.	*Competes for the air space.*
The complainer	Constantly whinges, whines or nags.	*Pollutes the air space.*
The enabler	Listens with empathy. Nurtures, encourages.	*Invites you to use your share of the air space.*
The explainer	Fills you in with every minuscule detail.	*Informs you how the air space works.*
The falterer	Has difficulty finding the right words (I don't know how to put it – know what I mean!)	*Hopes you will fill the gaps in the air space.*
The interferer	Has to have their five penn'orth (intrudes, meddles).	*Sticks their oar in the air space.*
The interrupter	Barges in, butts in.	*Cuts you off from your air space.*
The judger	Lectures, preaches, moralises, criticises.	*Tells you what you should do in the air space.*
The negotiator	Likes to settle disagreements. Is prepared to compromise. Conciliates, mediates.	*Works with you to make best use of the air space.*
The submitter	Says very little. Puts other people's needs first.	*Gives away their share of the air space.*

Fig. 13. A variety of communication styles.

3. In your communications with others, have you found yourself:

    - switching off?

    - trying to make a quick getaway?

    - wishing the person would change the record?

    - hearing only what you want to hear?

    - feeling bored, irritated, frustrated?

    Which of the styles generate these reactions in you?

4. There are three effective communication styles included in the list: the asserter, the enabler and the negotiator. Can you relate to these styles?

ENABLING COMMUNICATION TO GROW

There are three fundamental relationship qualities that form the roots of skilful communication:

1. *The ability to demonstrate respect for other people.* Showing respect enables people to feel accepted, heard, valued and important.

2. *The ability to be yourself* – to be real, genuine. Genuineness invites sincerity and encourages other people to be more open and honest in their communication with you.

3. *The ability to show empathy.* This means being able to understand things from the other person's perspective – to be alongside, to put yourself in the other person's shoes, to listen sensitively to their experiences without condemning or criticising, to choose the right time to respond, and to respond with the appropriate words.

Let us see how the asserter, enabler and negotiator demonstrate these qualities.

The asserter

Assertive people express their needs clearly and honestly. They stand up for their rights, and show respect for other people's needs and rights. They are genuine in their communication. They do not judge or blame others. They work towards achieving equal communication and win-win situations, where both parties feel respected, valued and important.

The enabler
Enablers listen empathetically to what other people have to say, and encourage people to express their thoughts and feelings openly and honestly. They do not pass judgements or make assumptions. They show respect for people and accept them for the unique human beings they are.

The negotiator
Negotiators may not necessarily agree with others. However, they show respect by listening to other people's opinions and feelings and by trying to understand things from the other person's perspective. They are willing to work towards a compromise, where both parties feel acknowledged.

Do you demonstrate these qualities in your interpersonal communications:

- respect
- genuineness
- empathy
- a non-judgemental attitude?

CONVEYING WARMTH AND BUILDING TRUST WILL NOURISH THE ROOTS OF SKILFUL COMMUNICATION

Showing warmth
An attitude of warmth is essential for communication to flourish. A cheery smile, welcoming tone, tender words, or words of praise and encouragement, kindness and hospitality, a reassuring hug, a peck on the cheek, touching a person's arm, holding their hand, or putting an arm round their shoulder, can generally melt even the most icy heart. **Touch is an extremely powerful form of communication**.

Building trust
Trust can be established by good listening, empathy, respect, genuineness, warmth, and acceptance. The more you invest in your communications, the greater the return you can expect. A relationship built on trust facilitates closeness and harmony.

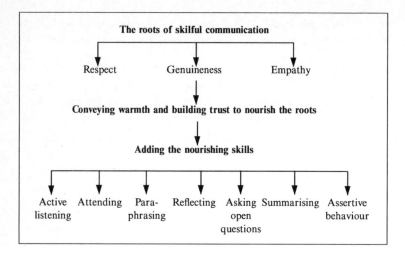

Fig. 14. Summary of the process of skilful communication.

ADDING THE NOURISHING SKILLS

By planting healthy roots, we are well on our way to achieving communication that is rewarding and satisfying. By adding a variety of nourishing skills we can ripen the fruits of communication and reap the harvest of a deeply enriching experience. Figure 14 summarises the process of skilful communication.

EXPLORING THE NOURISHING SKILLS

It is the province of knowledge to speak and it is the privilege of wisdom to listen.

(Oliver Wendell Holmes)

Identifying the components of active listening
Active listening involves:

- Giving the speaker our undivided time and attention.

- Listening with sensitivity and without interrupting the speaker.

- Listening with an open mind and suspending judgement.

- Listening to the meanings – what is possibly being felt but is not openly being expressed. This entails listening with our senses:

  – our ears to hear the words spoken, the rate of speech, the tone of voice, the volume, the pitch

  – our eyes to note the speaker's body-language, the gestures, facial expressions, posture, movements

  – our mind to sift through the meaning and to sort out how we are going to respond

  – ourselves – how we might feel if we were in the speaker's shoes.

- Resisting the temptation to break the speaker's silences, which allows the speaker time to collect their thoughts.

- Asking questions that encourage the flow of communication rather than closing it down.

- Remembering what the speaker has said (the better you listen – the better you hear – the more you remember – the better you understand).

- Remaining cool, calm and collected even though you may not feel like it.

- Responding appropriately.

> **Good listening is the key to skilful communication.**
> **It is one of the most priceless gifts we can offer other people. When a person feels listened to they feel accepted, valued, respected, heard and understood.**

Focusing on the components of attending
Good attending demonstrates that we are available to the speaker, both physically and emotionally. Attending involves:

- Maintaining appropriate eye contact.

- Adopting an open posture – facing the speaker, standing or sitting at a comfortable distance, leaning towards the speaker occasionally, mirroring the speaker's body language, tilting our head to one side to express interest and remaining relaxed.

- Using appropriate facial expressions that acknowledge the speaker's feelings.

- Speaking at an appropriate volume, using a suitable tone and focusing on the positive.

- Not hiding behind barriers – such as desks or tables, or folding our arms and crossing our legs.

- Not fidgeting about – for example, tapping our fingers on the arms of the chair, twisting a strand of hair, fiddling with items of clothing, shuffling our chair about, pointing our feet towards the door (which indicates we are ready to leave or have heard enough), or glancing at our watch.

- Using minimal encouragers to show that we are listening and to encourage the speaker to continue talking. Here are some examples:
  - Oh.
  - Tell me more.
  - Uh-huh.
  - Umm-hmmm.
  - I see. And then...?
  - That's interesting. Please go on ...
  - So ...
  - Ah-ah.
  - Silence (*Silence can be a valuable minimal encourager as it enables people to think, feel and express.*)

RESPONDING APPROPRIATELY

Choosing the right time to respond is important. Try and wait for a natural break in the conversation and watch the speaker's eyes. They can give you valuable clues about whether they are ready for you to respond.

There are a number of ways in which you can respond appropriately.

1. Paraphrasing content

This involves feeding back the significant points to ensure understanding. Paraphrasing communicates respect, builds trust and reduces distortion. Paraphrases need only be brief, and *tentative* – in case you have misunderstood. For example:

- What you seem to be saying is...
- What seems to be coming across is...

- It sounds as if ...
- What I am hearing is...
- So what you are saying is...
- So, it's as though you...
- In other words...

When you have finished paraphrasing, return to active listening. The speaker will correct any information you may have misinterpreted.

2. Reflecting feelings

Reflecting feelings involves feeding back the significant feelings to demonstrate that you have understood how the person is feeling. Reflecting feelings encourages the speaker to clarify the reasons for the feelings, conveys acceptance, builds trust and facilitates deeper understanding. Again, make your responses brief and *tentative*. Here are some examples:

- You feel...because...
- I seem to be picking up a feeling of...
- I'm also picking up that you feel...
- So you feel as if...
- This has left you feeling...
- And all this is leaving you feeling...

3. Asking open questions

Basically, there are two types of questions: open questions which help the flow of communication and encourage the speaker to elaborate or be more specific, and closed questions which tend to shut communication down. Closed questions are those that can be answered with a 'Yes' or 'No'. For example: Did you...? Do you think that...? Are you going to...? They are useful for seeking factual information.

Open questions begin with:

- **What?** For example, 'What happened exactly?'

- **How?** For example, 'How do you feel about what's happened?'

- **When?** For example, 'When you said... I wasn't quite sure what you meant exactly. Can you tell me a bit more?'

- **Where?** For example, 'Where would it be helpful to start?'

- **Who?** For example, 'Who else is involved in the situation?'

- **Would you?** For example, 'Would you care to elaborate on what you have just said?'

4. Summarising
Summarising involves pulling the threads of the speaker's communication together to check accurate understanding.

Here are some examples:

- Perhaps it might be helpful to summarise what you have said.
- Let's pull a few threads together here.
- Let me see if I have understood you correctly.
- If I can just recap.
- Let me check whether I have got things straight.

Knowing what to avoid
Avoid doing any of the following:

1. **Asking prying questions** – to satisfy your own curiosity.

2. **Asking *why* questions** – which can sound like an interrogation and tend to put people on the defensive, or make them feel as if they have got to justify their actions.

3. **Asking leading questions** – for example: 'Wouldn't you agree that your behaviour was...?'

4. **Making judgements** – for example: 'Surely with your vast experience, you could have...', 'Obviously, you could have...'. Listen to yourself when you hear yourself saying 'surely' or 'obviously'. These two words are often used to pass judgement.

5. **Giving uncalled for advice** – for example: 'If I were you I would...', 'What you should do is...'.

DEVELOPING ASSERTIVE BEHAVIOUR

Learning to behave more assertively leads to more fruitful communication and increased self-confidence.

Assertive people:

- Take responsibility for their thoughts, feelings and behaviour. They do not blame or judge others.

- Stand up for their rights, and respect the rights of other people.

- Act without undue fear or anxiety.

- Ask for what they want and need openly and honestly, and accept that they may not get exactly what they want. They do not fight to win their corner – unlike the aggressive person.

- Are willing to compromise or negotiate to settle conflict situations. They do not take flight from difficult situations, or allow themselves to be walked over – unlike the passive or submissive person.

- Don't feel the need to bully or manipulate others (unlike the aggressive person), and don't feel the need to please others in the hope they will be approved of (unlike the passive person).

- Can give and accept praise easily.

- Can give and accept criticism – they are aware of their particular 'crumple buttons' and do not over-react to criticism.

- Have high levels of self-confidence and self-esteem, and build other people's self-confidence and self-esteem.

- Like themselves for who they are, and accept other people as they are.

EXPLORING THE ADVANTAGES OF ASSERTIVENESS TRAINING

Assertiveness training courses are available at most adult education centres. Learning assertiveness techniques in a group situation can be fun and rewarding. Attending a course not only provides you with the opportunity to practise the skills in a safe environment, it also gives you an opportunity to share experiences, increase self-awareness and build on existing skills. Figure 15 shows a sample of my 12-week assertiveness training programme. From this you will see that many of the skills have been covered throughout this book. However, practising them with others can be a productive way to continue developing the skills, as well as raising self-confidence and self-esteem.

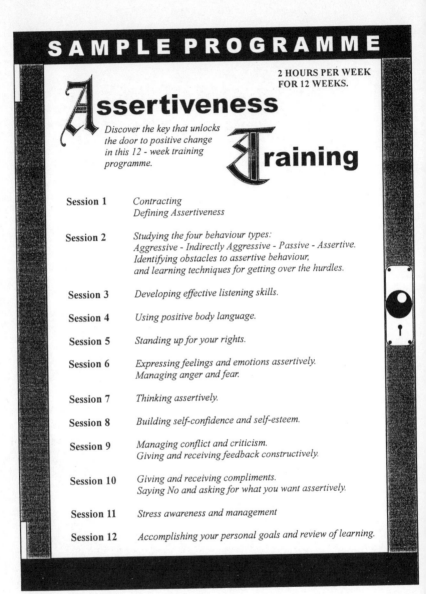

SAMPLE PROGRAMME

2 HOURS PER WEEK
FOR 12 WEEKS.

Assertiveness

*Discover the key that unlocks
the door to positive change
in this 12 - week training
programme.*

Training

Session 1	*Contracting* *Defining Assertiveness*
Session 2	*Studying the four behaviour types:* *Aggressive - Indirectly Aggressive - Passive - Assertive.* *Identifying obstacles to assertive behaviour,* *and learning techniques for getting over the hurdles.*
Session 3	*Developing effective listening skills.*
Session 4	*Using positive body language.*
Session 5	*Standing up for your rights.*
Session 6	*Expressing feelings and emotions assertively.* *Managing anger and fear.*
Session 7	*Thinking assertively.*
Session 8	*Building self-confidence and self-esteem.*
Session 9	*Managing conflict and criticism.* *Giving and receiving feedback constructively.*
Session 10	*Giving and receiving compliments.* *Saying No and asking for what you want assertively.*
Session 11	*Stress awareness and management*
Session 12	*Accomplishing your personal goals and review of learning.*

Fig. 15. Sample 12-week assertiveness training programme.

CASE STUDY 13 – REVISITING WOUND-UP WENDY AND LAID-BACK LAWRENCE

Clearing the air

This case study picks up from Case Study 6 (Chapter 3), where we looked at how Wendy and Lawrence were experiencing problems as a result of poor communication. The aim of revisiting Wendy and Lawrence is to look at how different the picture could be if they learned to communicate more effectively.

Starting with breakfast time

Lawrence tunes in to Wendy's sighing and puffing (he reads the situation).

Lawrence: Wendy, you seem flustered, what can I do to help? (showing respect and asking an open question)

Wendy: I do feel under pressure, and would appreciate some help. (owning feelings and stating her needs) There's several things that need doing before I leave for work.

Lawrence: Can you tell me specifically what needs doing? (open question)

Wendy: Well, there's the beds to be made, the kids' sandwiches to prepare, the breakfast things to wash up, and the bin needs putting out. (clarifying)

Lawrence: I can see that you have a lot to do. (being empathetic) Perhaps if I prepare the kids' sandwiches and wash up it might take a bit of the pressure off you. How does that sound?

Wendy: That sounds great to me. Thanks for offering.

Moving on to tea-time

Lawrence arrives home.

Wendy: I feel absolutely exhausted. (expressing feelings)

Lawrence: I've had a pretty horrendous day myself, but I can see how shattered you are. Go and sit yourself down and I'll make us a nice cup of tea. Then I'll give you a hand to prepare the dinner. (being empathetic and putting his own needs aside)

Wendy: Thank you. (accepts his gift) You say you've had a ghastly day. (paraphrasing) What's been so awful about it? (open question)

Lawrence:	I don't want to bore you.
Wendy:	I won't be bored – I'm all ears. (giving an open invitation to talk and expressing interest)

Moving on now to the evening when the children have gone to bed

Lawrence:	Wendy, you seem to be getting wound up a lot lately, and I'm wondering whether you would like to talk about what's causing it? (open question)
Wendy:	You're right. I have been feeling stressed out (expressing feeling)... I guess it's because.... (pauses)
Lawrence:	Go on, I'm listening. (attending)
Wendy:	Well, I guess I'm struggling to keep on top of things – what with Rebecca, the kids and going back to work. I also feel... a bit... angry with.... (pauses)
Lawrence:	Angry with? (reflecting feeling and minimal encourager)
Wendy:	I feel angry with you (expressing feeling) because I think you could do more to help. (gives reason)
Lawrence:	I didn't realise you felt like that, and I'm glad you've told me. So you feel as if I'm not pulling my weight as much as I could? (paraphrasing)
Wendy:	That's right. (indicates that Lawrence has hit the nail on the head!)

Wendy and Lawrence continue to share the air space to discuss how they can resolve the situation.

Moving on to bedtime

Wendy:	I'm really pleased you brought things out into the open, and we've been able to clear the air between us. I feel better already. (expressing feelings)
Lawrence:	I'm pleased too. It's made me feel a lot happier. (expressing feelings)
Wendy:	Shall we go to bed? I could really do with a cuddle. (stating needs)
Lawrence:	Sounds like a good idea to me. I feel in need of a cuddle too. (stating needs)

As we can see, we no longer have a wound-up Wendy or laid-back Lawrence. We have more of a **Listening Lawrence** and a **Warmed-up Wendy**, which goes to show how relationships can be greatly enriched by fruitful communication.

Marriage is a framework to preserve friendship. It is valuable because it gives more room to develop than just living together. It provides a base from which a person can work at understanding himself and another person.

(Robertson Davies)

KEEPING YOUR PERSONAL DEVELOPMENT JOURNAL

A still tongue makes a wise head.

(Proverb)

1. Identify a situation in your life that is causing conflict. Write down the cause of the conflict from your point of view. Think about the other person(s) involved. Try and put yourself in their shoes.

    - How do you think they view the situation?

    - Note your thoughts and feelings about the situation.

    - Ask yourself: Would I feel better if I tried to resolve this conflict?

    - If your answer is yes, ask yourself: What action can I take to resolve this conflict?

   Note: If you find this difficult, try using a goal-setting approach (see Chapter 9).

2. Record any specific skills you need to develop that could help you communicate more skilfully, together with details of how you could go about developing these skills (*eg* enrolling on a course).

   Note: The skills demonstrated here are taught to trainee counsellors. If they have stimulated your taste buds and you would like to learn more about them (plus advanced skills), you could benefit from reading *Learning to Counsel – How to Develop the Skills to Work Effectively With Others*, by Jan Sutton and William Stewart (available from How To Books – see Further Reading section).

7

Raising Your Self-esteem

We can secure other people's approval, if we do right and try hard; but our own is worth a hundred of it.

(Mark Twain)

Raising self-esteem is a vital factor in learning to thrive on stress. If we possess high self-esteem we feel good about who we are. We don't hide behind a mask of self-doubt or insecurity. We can take criticism in our stride, don't get overwhelmed by feelings, and are less likely to over-react to stressful situations.

ELABORATING ON SELF-ESTEEM

Self-esteem is the reputation we acquire with ourselves.

(Nathaniel Branden)

Self-esteem can be defined as the view we hold of ourselves. If we see ourselves in a positive light, believing we are a person of value and worth, and have high self-regard, we possess a healthy measure of built-in self-esteem. On the other hand, if we view ourselves in a negative light, believing we are of little or no value, and have low self-regard, we have an absence of built-in self-esteem.

It's what's on the inside that counts

People with low self-esteem go to extraordinary lengths to feel better about themselves – they may spend a fortune on designer clothes or cosmetic surgery, or adorn themselves with masses of expensive jewellery or make-up. They half-heartedly accept compliments others give them, not really believing them, because deep down on the inside they don't believe in themselves, and it's what's on the inside that counts.

Viewing the two sides of self-esteem

People with high self-esteem	People with low self-esteem
• Like and approve of themselves exactly as they are.	• Dislike and disapprove of themselves. They seek approval from others by trying hard to please.
• Like to be liked, but it's not the end of the world if they aren't. They accept that it's not realistic to expect everyone to like them.	• Need to be liked.
• Have a good self-image.	• Have a poor self-image.
• Accept themselves – warts-and-all.	• Reject themselves.
• Talk positively to themselves.	• Talk negatively to themselves.
• Don't give themselves a hard time if they make a mistake. They criticise their *behaviour*.	• Beat themselves up if they make a mistake. They criticise *themselves*.
• Can handle criticism.	• Can be devastated by criticism, *because it reinforces their self-beliefs that they are useless, hopeless, stupid, thick.*
• Focus on their strengths.	• Focus on their weaknesses.
• Are assertive – they stand up for themselves.	• Tend to be passive (*they let people walk all over them*), or they bully people (*to bolster their low self-esteem*).
• Are independent people.	• Are dependent people.

Basically, people with high self-esteem treat themselves kindly, which makes them feel good about themselves, which leads to positive action and success. People with low self-esteem tend to denigrate themselves, believing they don't deserve, or will never be good enough, which leads to negative actions and distress.

IDENTIFYING THE LINKS BETWEEN LOW SELF-ESTEEM AND MIND-TALK

One of the primary aims of this book has been to emphasise how our mind-talk affects our feelings and actions. People with low self-esteem are filled with negative mind-talk such as: 'I'm absolutely useless, hopeless, thick, stupid, a waste of space'. Negative mind-talk is one of the major obstacles to overcoming low self-esteem. People with low self-esteem need to internalise new messges about themselves, positive messages, self-nurturing messages, for example, 'I am a worthwhile person, I am worth loving, I am just as good as the next person'. Becoming aware of, and constantly challenging negative mind-talk, is vital to building self-esteem.

Self-esteem and illness
Low self-esteem is frequently at the root of stress and depression, because people with low self-esteem have a negative view of themselves and a negative view of the world they live in.

EXPLORING THE ROOTS OF SELF-ESTEEM

The seeds of self-esteem are firmly planted in childhood. If we are blessed with parents or carers who view the nurturing of self-esteem as high priority, we begin to develop a high level of built-in self-worth. On the other hand, if we are less fortunate, growing up in an environment where parents or carers fail to nourish our self-esteem, we begin to develop a low sense of self-worth. Children with high self-esteem are loved unconditionally – for **being** the unique individuals they are, with all their faults and failings. They develop the skills of self-nurturing. Children with low self-esteem tend to be loved conditionally – for **doing** or **achieving**. They fail to learn the skills of self-nurturing.

People with low self-esteem are hungry for approval
People whose self-esteem has not been nurtured in early childhood are hungry for approval, eager to please, dependent on the opinions of others and vulnerable to criticism. They may spend their entire lives striving to win unconditional love by **doing** or **achieving**. Remember 'A' type Alan (Case Study 4 in Chapter 2)? He spent 38 years of his life trying to win his parents' unconditional love by **doing** and **achieving**.

Low self-esteem can be passed on
Low self-esteem can be transgenerational unless someone in a family recognises the destruction it causes and takes action to change the 'family blueprint'. Nobody teaches us to be parents, and sadly, if we

have not learnt the skills of healthy self-nurturing, we do not possess the skills to pass on this precious gift to our children.

Identifying the effects of childhood abuse, neglect and deprivation on self-esteem

Children who have been psychologically damaged through physical, emotional or sexual abuse, neglect or deprivation, often develop chronic low self-esteem. They have been starved of love and affection, or violated at the hands of adults, which leaves them with no idea of how to nurture themselves, and often deeply distrusting of adults or authority figures. They may also believe they deserved to be ill-treated or abused – convincing themselves they must be bad people. These unfortunate children are the casualties of life, they suffer unbearable emotional pain. They need long-term help and support from a wise and empathetic counsellor or psychologist, who will show them unconditional love, and who has the ability to plant the right conditions for their self-esteem to grow and flourish.

CASE STUDY 14 – ABUSED ANGELA

Angela had been sexually, physically and emotionally abused as a child. She had grown up believing she was stupid, useless, evil, awful, a bad girl – messages which her abuser had 'given her'. Angela was filled with self-hate and could see nothing good about herself. She attended counselling for a long time, and it took a lot of hard work for her to see herself as being of any value. Eventually, she was able to see that the abuse was not her fault, she was not responsible, and she started to feel more OK about herself. It was a gradual and lengthy process, but bit by bit she began to internalise a new and important belief about herself: 'I am a worthwhile person'.

> If rejection destroys your self-esteem, you're letting others hold you as an emotional hostage.
>
> (Brian Tracy)

Observing two different children's self-esteem developing

To demonstrate how children's self-esteem develops, let us compare two different scenarios.

Child one

A little boy is playing with a toy. Suddenly he gets frustrated because he cannot understand how the toy works. His mother stops what she is doing and says to her son: 'Here, let me help you'. She explains to her son how the toy works, and offers words of encouragement such as: 'Well done, that's good, you're doing really well'. If we observed the look on this child's face we would probably see an expression of delight – the child would feel good about himself and good about what he had achieved.

This child internalises his experience. He believes:

- I am a capable and worthwhile person.

- Mummy accepts me even though I am not perfect.

- I am important.

Child two

A little girl is playing with a toy. Suddenly she gets frustrated because she cannot understand how the toy works. Her mother stops what she is doing grudgingly and snatches the toy from the child. She says: 'For goodness sake, let me do it, you're absolutely useless – nothing but a nuisance'. If we observed the look on this child's face we would probably see an expression of hurt – the child would feel bad about herself, and bad about not being able to get the toy to work.

This child internalises her experience. She believes:

- I am a useless person.

- I'm nothing but a nuisance.

- I must try harder to please Mummy, otherwise she might give up on me.

- I'm nothing special.

Let's move on to when these two children are at school.

Child one

The teacher asks the little boy to write a story about his holiday. She reads what he has written and praises him with: 'That was excellent'. He then takes his story home, eager to show his parents. They respond to him with: 'That's brilliant. You're a very clever lad and we are proud of you.' This does wonders for the little boy's self-esteem. He feels prized, valued and even more worthwhile. He shows all the signs of healthy self-esteem.

Child two
The teacher asks the little girl to draw a picture of where she went on holiday. She looks at the little girl's picture and criticises it: 'That's not very good, you'll never make an artist'. The little girl takes the picture home, and reluctantly shows it to her parents. They respond with: 'What on earth is that supposed to be – you're hopeless at art. Why can't you be more like your sister? She's brilliant at art.' This deflates the little girl's already fragile self-esteem and reinforces her belief: 'I'm useless, I'll never be good enough'. She feels rejected and worthless. She shows all the signs of low self-esteem.

Summary
The case study and examples highlight how our self-esteem is shaped by our parents and other authority figures, such as teachers. Grandparents, peers and siblings can also play a significant part. Being compared with a brother or sister can be very damaging to a child's self-esteem.

BUILDING UP LOW SELF-ESTEEM

Building up low self-esteem can seem like a formidable task, because it means working from the inside out. It means getting to the roots of negative self-beliefs and digging them out. It then necessitates planting new and healthy self-beliefs which need to be nurtured in order to become sturdy and flourish. Seeds don't blossom into beautiful flowers unless they receive tender loving care and attention. Other people can guide us in the right direction, but ultimately it's down to us to plant our own healthy seeds, and to nourish them so they grow into an exquisite flower.

Smoothing over the cracks
Journeying through life is rarely like travelling on a smooth and straight motorway. For many of us, it's more like traversing country lanes with twists and turns and bumps in the road. Nobody gets through life without having to face some trauma, such as the loss of a loved one through death, separation or divorce. Any major loss can cause cracks to appear in our self-esteem. However, with self-

determination and adequate support, it's possible to smooth over the cracks and recover our self-esteem.

CASE STUDY 15 – DEVOTED DEIRDRE

> Doubt whom you will, but never doubt yourself.
>
> (Christian Nestell Bovee)

Deirdre had devoted a large part of her life to looking after her home and bringing up her children. When her youngest son left home to go to university she was devastated. Her whole purpose for living diminished overnight. She felt no longer needed or valued. Her self-esteem and sense of identity had been completely wrapped up in her children, and without them around to take care of she saw herself as a nobody and became depressed. Deirdre sought counselling. When the counsellor asked her to identify her strengths she struggled to come up with any. She believed that because she had been out of the workplace for many years she had no skills to offer. She described herself as 'just a housewife and mother'. This was a self put-down. However, when encouraged to focus on what skills she had acquired through being a housewife and mother, she was able to identify the following:

- She kept a neat and orderly home.
- She cooked nutritious meals on a limited budget.
- She was a good friend to her children and their friends. She listened to their problems.
- She encouraged her children's learning.
- She decorated the home.
- She maintained the garden.

Having identified these strengths, the counsellor then asked her to focus on her forgotten childhood ambitions – the things she had put on hold while she was raising her family. Deirdre had always dreamed of owning and running a tea shop. When she explored further the skills she had developed through bringing up a family and looking after a home, she began to see that this ambition might still be achievable. She became excited at the prospect, and as the seeds of her idea grew so did her confidence and self-esteem. She started to believe in herself again, and began looking after her own needs. Within a short space of time she found that she enjoyed the freedom of being able to pursue her goal. A year later Deirdre had converted her conservatory into a small tea room, and her spare bedrooms into guest rooms so she could offer bed and breakfast.

Needless to say, Deirdre felt delighted about what she had achieved, and her self-confidence and self-esteem continued to grow in leaps and bounds.

Deirdre's counsellor might have planted the seeds for self-confidence and healthy esteem to develop, but it was Deirdre herself who put in all the hard work to foster their growth.

Summarising self-esteem

- Self-esteem is the beliefs we hold about ourselves. These may be high, low or somewhere in between.

- The roots of self-esteem are based in childhood experiences. Healthy seeds promote healthy growth; unhealthy seeds stunt growth.

  There is overwhelming evidence that the higher the level of self-esteem, the more likely one will treat others with respect, kindness, and generosity. People who do not experience self-love have little or no capacity to love others.

  (Nathaniel Branden)

PLANTING THE SEEDS FOR HEALTHY GROWTH

What is a weed? A plant whose virtues have not been discovered.

(Ralph Waldo Emerson)

Building self-confidence can positively enhance self-esteem. The following activities are designed to encourage you on your journey to improved self-confidence and increased self-esteem. My hope is they will provide you with the seeds, which you will continue to nurture.

ACTIVITY 21 – Establishing your current level of self-esteem

To establish a picture of your current level of self-esteem, rank yourself on a scale of 1–5 on the following chart, 5 being the highest score. There are no right or wrong answers.

I believe I am a worthwhile person	1	2	3	4	5
I accept myself for who I am	1	2	3	4	5
I praise myself on my achievements	1	2	3	4	5
I have faith in my abilities	1	2	3	4	5
I achieve my life goals	1	2	3	4	5
I see myself in a positive light	1	2	3	4	5
I accept that it's OK to make mistakes	1	2	3	4	5
I believe I am as good as the next person	1	2	3	4	5
I see myself as confident	1	2	3	4	5
I acknowledge my strengths	1	2	3	4	5
I can take criticism	1	2	3	4	5
I respect myself	1	2	3	4	5
I reward myself for the good things I do	1	2	3	4	5
I am not afraid to take risks	1	2	3	4	5
I accept that not everyone will like me	1	2	3	4	5
I give praise and encouragement to others	1	2	3	4	5
I set myself realistic goals	1	2	3	4	5
I seek support when I need it	1	2	3	4	5
I act rather than react	1	2	3	4	5
I don't strive to be perfect	1	2	3	4	5
I give and accept compliments	1	2	3	4	5
I focus on my successes not my failures	1	2	3	4	5
I like being with positive people	1	2	3	4	5

Look back over the scores you have assigned yourself. A very high score indicates a healthy level of self-esteem, whereas a low score means you need to do some considerable work to build your self-esteem. Record any low scores in your journal under the heading 'areas I need to work on'.

ACTIVITY 22 – Identifying your personal qualities

What do you most like about yourself?

Rank yourself on a scale of 1–5 on the following chart, 5 being the highest score. Again, there are no right or wrong answers.

I see myself as:

kind	1	2	3	4	5
reliable	1	2	3	4	5
helpful	1	2	3	4	5
loyal	1	2	3	4	5
caring	1	2	3	4	5
friendly	1	2	3	4	5
approachable	1	2	3	4	5
positive	1	2	3	4	5
tolerant	1	2	3	4	5
understanding	1	2	3	4	5
compassionate	1	2	3	4	5
honest	1	2	3	4	5
fair	1	2	3	4	5
non-judgemental	1	2	3	4	5
efficient	1	2	3	4	5
organised	1	2	3	4	5
sincere	1	2	3	4	5
happy	1	2	3	4	5
confident	1	2	3	4	5
assertive	1	2	3	4	5
calm	1	2	3	4	5
attractive	1	2	3	4	5
intelligent	1	2	3	4	5
sympathetic	1	2	3	4	5
empathetic	1	2	3	4	5
an effective communicator	1	2	3	4	5
a good listener	1	2	3	4	5
adaptable	1	2	3	4	5
conscientious	1	2	3	4	5
decisive	1	2	3	4	5
a good problem-solver	1	2	3	4	5
patient	1	2	3	4	5
competent	1	2	3	4	5
creative	1	2	3	4	5
talented	1	2	3	4	5

Look back over the scores you have assigned yourself. Record in your journal any scores you would like to see higher, under the heading 'room for improvement'.

ACTIVITY 23 – Focusing on your personal achievements

What have you achieved that you are proud of?

Make a list of all your achievements, for example:

- school achievements
- work achievements
- sports and hobbies
- artistic/creative talents
- home/family activities
- relationships
- community activities.

Out of all these personal achievements, which ones fill you with the most pride?

ACTIVITY 24 – Identifying your positive attributes

What are you skilled at?

Look at the examples given in Figure 16 and then brainstorm your own list. Brainstorming means jotting down any thoughts that come into your head. One thought can often trigger another, so it is a useful technique for generating a free flow of thoughts. Don't be coy when doing this activity. It's a valuable opportunity to blow your own trumpet – something we are rarely encouraged to do. Try using 'I' statements, thereby owning your positive attributes.

GIVING AND RECEIVING COMPLIMENTS

> I will praise any man that will praise me.
>
> (Shakespeare)

Being able to give and receive compliments is a wonderful way to build self-esteem. The more compliments we give, the more we tend to get back. Relationships can be positively enriched by the giving and receiving of compliments. However, it is important that any compliments given are sincere, otherwise they can come across as patronising. An insincere compliment can be spotted a mile off.

If we have not been used to receiving compliments we may feel embarrassed and reject the compliment.

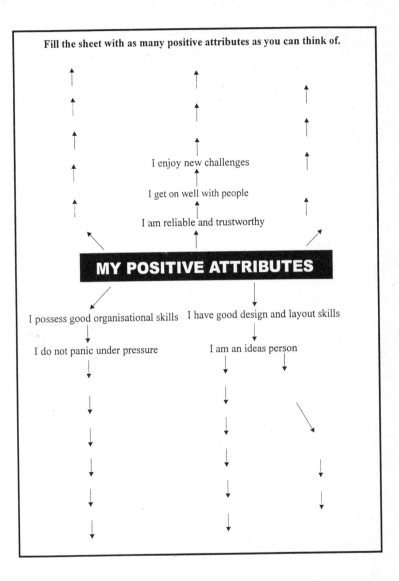

Fill the sheet with as many positive attributes as you can think of.

I enjoy new challenges

I get on well with people

I am reliable and trustworthy

MY POSITIVE ATTRIBUTES

I possess good organisational skills

I have good design and layout skills

I do not panic under pressure

I am an ideas person

Fig. 16. Example of a brainstorm – identifying your positive attributes.

Examples
- Compliment: 'I really like that dress you are wearing.'
  Rejection: *'What, this old thing? I've had it for years.'*

- Compliment: 'I think you are a very special person.'
  Rejection: *'Don't say that, you're making me blush.'*

- Compliment: 'I think you have done an excellent job.'
  Rejection: *'It's OK, but I expect you could have done it better.'*

Rejecting compliments means in effect we are handing them back, and the chances are that if we continue to reject them they will soon stop coming. We don't get too many so savour them, believe them and internalise them. All you need to respond with is something like: 'Thank you' or 'I'm pleased you like it'.

When giving compliments the most direct way to give them is to say: 'I think you are/have...', 'I feel you are...', 'I like your...'. Using 'I' statements means you are taking personal responsibility for the compliment.

IDENTIFYING A WINNING HAND

I can live for two months on a good compliment

(Mark Twain)

Unconditional compliments

These are compliments that come straight from the heart, and they warm the heart of the receiver. If we compare them to the aces in a pack of cards, they could be viewed as the ace of hearts. Ace of hearts compliments say something about you as a person (without any strings attached). They are the most priceless gifts we can give or receive.

Examples of ace of hearts compliments:
- I think you are wonderful.
- I think you are beautiful.
- I think you are very handsome.
- I admire you as a person.
- I love you just the way you are.
- I think you are magic.
- There's nothing about you I would like to change.
- I think you are perfect.
- You are the most fascinating person I have ever come across.

Conditional compliments

Conditional compliments are also valuable gifts to give or receive. They could be viewed as the ace of diamonds. Ace of diamonds compliments say something about who you are, or what you do. Adults appreciate receiving conditional compliments – they like being praised for something they have done well.

Examples of ace of diamonds compliments:
- I think you are excellent at your job.
- I think you have written a very good essay.
- I think you are a very kind person.
- I value your comments.
- I appreciate your friendship.
- I think you have good dress sense.
- I like you new hairstyle.
- I love that jacket you are wearing.
- I think you are an excellent hostess.
- I think you deserve to come top after all the hard work you have put in.

The ace of hearts and the ace of diamonds could both be viewed as a **winning hand**.

IDENTIFYING A LOSING HAND

The two remaining aces in a pack of cards could be viewed as negative criticisms.

Ace of spades criticisms

Dealing the ace of spades is like '**having a dig**' at a person. These negative criticisms are often disguised in the form of humour or sarcasm.

Examples of ace of spades criticisms:
- Are you wearing that for a bet?
- Where did you get that outfit from – a charity shop?
- Oh, well done. It's really good of you to grace us with your presence.
- Remind me not to go to the same hairdresser as you!
- If you had brains, you'd be dangerous!

The person who deals out ace of spades criticisms uses indirect aggression. Receiving ace of spades criticisms can hurt – they hit home like a sniper's bullet. The best way to deal with them is by shrugging them off – we don't have to accept the cards we're dealt.

Ace of clubs criticisms
Dealing ace of clubs criticisms is like dealing a deadly blow. Ace of clubs criticisms destroy a person's self-confidence and self-esteem.

Examples of Ace of clubs criticisms:
- You are stupid, useless, hopeless, thick, a waste of space.
- You'll never make anything of yourself.
- If only you were like your brother – at least he's got a bit of common sense.
- I wish you'd never been born.
- I knew it would be a mistake having another girl.

Being on the receiving end is like being dealt a **club over the head**. Sadly, if these criticisms are dealt out too often, the receiver internalises them and believes them to be fact.

THROWING AWAY A LOSING HAND

No one can make you feel inferior without your consent.
(Eleanor Roosevelt)

We may believe that we don't stand a chance of becoming a winner because we have been dealt a losing hand. However, there's nothing stopping us from throwing away our losing hand and dealing ourselves some aces of hearts and aces of diamonds. It's a great starting point for building self-esteem.

CASE STUDY 16 – TRIUMPHANT TERRY

The childhood shows the man, as morning shows the day.
(John Milton)

Terry was the youngest of four children. He had two sisters and a brother. His brother (the blue-eyed boy of the family) was 16 years older than Terry, and his sisters (twins) were 14 years his senior. Terry's parents had not wanted any more children after the twins, and his mother frequently let Terry know this by saying: 'I wish you'd never been born – you were a mistake'. In Terry's young and impressionable mind he internalised this as: 'I should never have been born, my mother doesn't want me, I must be unlovable'.

Terry feels unwanted

Terry's father was rarely at home. He spent his evenings in the pub, arriving home drunk and ready to pick a fight. Many nights Terry would lie awake in bed listening to his parents arguing. His name came up in almost every argument, each parent blaming the problems of their marriage on Terry. Father would say: 'It's your fault I go drinking, you knew I didn't want any more children'. Mother would retaliate with: 'I didn't want any more either, and I'm the one who is saddled with him while you're out enjoying yourself'.

Terry wishes he'd never been born

Terry felt very hurt and rejected, believing he was to blame for his parents' problems – after all, his parents wouldn't say it if it wasn't true. He began to wish he had never been born. He felt very alone and unhappy. Terry could not talk to anyone about how he felt. His 'blue-eyed' brother was away at college, and his sisters had little time for their 'baby brother'. His mother was preoccupied with her own problems and suffered from bouts of depression. His father only ever spoke to him through a haze of alcohol, and when he did it was usually to criticise something Terry had done. He was constantly being compared with his brother with words such as: 'Why can't you be like your brother – you're a loser – you'll never amount to anything'. There was also an 'unspoken family law' that it was not permissible to talk about feelings or express opinions.

Terry becomes invisible

Terry suffered in silence, trying everything within his power to please his parents, but nothing worked. To avoid the constant barrage of criticism he became almost 'invisible', spending most of his time in his bedroom.

Terry gets bullied at school

At school he got little respite from his emotional pain. He was a slight lad and wore glasses. The school bullies had a field day with him, constantly tormenting him with cruel remarks such as 'weedy' or 'four eyes'. In his desperation to be accepted he tried to shrug off these hurtful digs, but they invariably hit their target, and further reduced his already fragile self-esteem. No matter what he did, or how hard he tried, Terry never felt accepted. He viewed himself as a misfit – a victim of society.

Terry rebels

His years of inner turmoil erupted in his teens. He'd received no love, affection or attention through being a 'good' or 'invisible' child, so he changed his strategy. He became a rebel – regularly playing truant from school, believing that this might make his parents sit up and give him some attention. Letters started arriving from the headteacher threatening to expel Terry if he didn't 'pull his socks up' and Terry got caught in the crossfire of arguments between his parents. His father blamed his mother: 'This is all your fault', and his mother blamed his father: 'You've never shown any interest in him'. Both dumped the blame on Terry for being such a useless waste of space. It did get him a bit of attention, albeit negative attention, but even negative attention was better than nothing. Neither parent asked: 'Why don't you want to go to school?'

Terry makes friends with the bottle

Terry's very fragile self-esteem started to reach rock-bottom. He had no real friends, his parents never listened to him, and he believed he was worthless and incapable of making anything of himself. When he was 13 he took his first drink – a strong can of lager which he stole from his father's secret supplies. This made him feel a bit better – it temporarily took away some of his inner pain. He continued to steal the odd can, seeing drink as the answer to his problems. It became his friend and comforter, anaesthetising the anguish that was festering away inside him. By the age of 15 Terry had become dependent on his 'friend' the drink, as a way of escaping from his inner torment and suffering. He stole bottles of whisky from the local supermarket, and money from his mum's purse to support his habit.

Terry tries buying friendship

Terry left school without gaining any qualifications. He couldn't get a job. This further reinforced his beliefs about himself – he was a useless waste of space. He felt very alone in a cruel and frightening world, and tried to buy friendship by treating the lads at the local pub. But when his money ran out, even they deserted him just like everyone else had done.

Terry steals to feed his habit
Terry drifted on aimlessly. His stealing habit escalated to feed his increasing dependency on alcohol. He got careless, and was caught red-handed by a store detective with a bottle of whisky he had stolen. He was frog-marched down to the local police station. The policeman who charged him gave him a gentle but firm talking to: 'Let this be a lesson to you my lad, if you carry on the way you're going you're heading for big problems. Do you really want to screw your life up? If you're worried about your drinking I can give you a leaflet about an organisation that can help you.' Terry sheepishly accepted the leaflet.

Terry glimpses a ray of hope
For several weeks the policeman's words kept popping up in Terry's mind. One day he plucked up courage to 'phone the number on the leaflet. He felt very apprehensive but breathed a huge sigh of relief when a warm and friendly voice thanked him for calling and invited him to attend a meeting. On six occasions Terry got as far as the door of the building where the meetings took place, but he couldn't summon up the courage to actually go in. One evening when he was 'hovering' around outside, a man spoke to him: 'Hi, you look lost, son – can I help you?' Terry was caught by surprise and didn't know what to say. The man introduced himself and said: 'You look as if you are in need of some company. Come on in and meet the group.' Terry warmed to the man, and followed him into a room where about a dozen men and women were sitting around chatting happily away to each other. They all smiled warmly at Terry and welcomed him to the meeting.

Terry plucks up the courage to share his experiences
Initially Terry found the meetings strange and daunting. Men and women from all walks of life stood up and openly shared their life experiences and the problems they had with drink. Terry felt very vulnerable and exposed, and sat through several meetings without saying a word. Nobody pressurised him. Gradually he gained the courage to speak. He felt 'choked' as he tried to put his life story into words, and fought hard to hold back his tears. The men and women in the group listened without interrupting. When he had finished speaking he felt as if the weight of the world had suddenly been lifted from his shoulders. There were no words of criticism, only words of understanding and compassion. For the first time in his life Terry had found a place of comfort, a place where he was

accepted unconditionally, a place where he could fit in.

Terry starts to believe in himself

This unconditional acceptance by the group members helped Terry to start believing in himself. He stopped drinking and soon became an active and valued member of the group. He started going out voluntarily to youth clubs and schools giving talks to teenagers about the dangers of alcohol. This did wonders for his self-confidence and self-esteem, as well as giving him a purpose in life. With continued support from the group members, Terry was also encouraged to take up a career in the helping professions. Their confidence in him gave him confidence in himself, and when he was old enough he applied to train as a probation officer.

Terry's self-esteem builds

After successfully completing his training, Terry chose to work with young offenders. He loves his work and feels of value to society. He likes the person he has become. His greatest reward is being able to give the lads the benefit of his experiences, and to show them that there is a way out of a life of crime if they can start to believe in themselves.

Terry knows only too well that the 'childhood shows the man' as John Milton wrote. However, he has also learnt some valuable lessons:

- It's never too late to change the childhood blueprint.
- There's no gain without pain.

Terry was definitely dealt the ace of clubs as a child, but he is living proof that it's possible to throw a losing hand away, and change it for a winning hand. He is no longer tormented Terry – his self-esteem is high – he is triumphant Terry.

> What lies behind us and what lies before us are tiny matters compared with what lies within us.
>
> (Ralph Waldo Emerson)

CASE STUDY 17 – RECOVERING RITA

Following the break-up of her marriage and problems at work, Rita suffered a bout of stress and depression, and was signed off sick by her GP. Rita's self-esteem was at an all time low. She used her time off constructively to devise her own 12-step recovery programme.

Step 1. Practise relaxation routines twice a day, once in the morning and once before I go to bed.

Step 2. Look after my health and pay attention to my diet. Do some form of exercise for 20 minutes each day.

Step 3. Find a counsellor to help me work through the grief of losing my husband.

Step 4. Enrol on a stress management course.

Step 5. Enrol on an assertiveness course.

Step 6. Keep a daily journal. Record my thoughts and feelings and practise challenging my negative mind-talk. Monitor daily progress.

Step 7. Go the library and borrow books on stress, assertiveness, conflict management and communication skills.

Step 8. Make a priority list of problems in my life and develop a problem-solving approach to tackling them.

Step 9. Develop peace of mind and spirituality. Purchase some meditation tapes and practise the techniques.

Step 10. Build a support network. Join a club. Make new friends and let people into my life.

Step 11. Set myself some realistic goals for the future, and work towards achieving them.

Step 12. Accept that it's OK not to be perfect. Learn to respect myself for who I am. Validate my successes and be kind to myself. Treat myself to something special for all my hard work and believe that I deserve a treat.

KEEPING YOUR PERSONAL DEVELOPMENT JOURNAL

Self-confidence is the first requisite to great undertakings.

(Samuel Johnson)

1. Record what action you could take to continue building your self-esteem.

2. Make a list of people you would like to give a compliment to.

Plan what you want to say, say it, and make a note of how it was received.

3. Make a complete list of all your positive qualities and each day practise affirming yourself out loud in front of a mirror, using 'I' statements. For example:

'I am a kind and thoughtful person.'

'I am a worthwhile person.'

'I am a likeable person.'

'I am a responsible person.'

'It's OK to express my opinions.'

'I am not to blame for what happened to me as a child.'

'It's OK to be myself.'

'I deserve to be happy.'

'I value who I am.'

'I trust myself.'

Keep repeating the affirmations until you believe them. And remember:

To love onself is the beginning of a lifelong romance.

(Oscar Wilde)

8

Mastering the Clock

To choose time is to save time.

(Francis Bacon)

Time is a valuable and sometimes scarce resource, and needs to be budgeted wisely. How often do you sit back and evaluate how you spend your time? Much unwelcome stress arises from packing too much into every minute of every day, or by wishing time away.

Do you hear yourself saying:

- I'd love to but I never have the time.
- I can't because I must get this finished.
- I'll have to cancel, I've got too much to do.
- I never have a spare minute.
- Oh God, I'm running out of time!
- There's never enough hours in the day.
- I wish it was time to go home.
- Why do today what I can put off 'til tomorrow?

Too much activity can lead to over-stimulation and exhaustion. Too little can lead to under-stimulation and frustration. Either can lead us on the path to stress. If the above statements sound familiar, it's time to 'stop the clock' and explore whether you are spending your time wisely.

WHAT IS TIME?

There are 24 hours in a day, 168 hours in a week, and 8,736 hours in an average year. If we live three score years and ten, we have approximately 611,520 hours on this earth. We have no control over time. However, we do have control of how we manage our time. **Are you master of your time?**

UNDERSTANDING HOW WE STRUCTURE TIME

Basically, we structure our time in seven different ways:

1. Serving time	This is committed time – the time we give to our work – our employers, committees, *etc*.
2. Domicile time	This is the time we spend at home – the time we devote to daily rituals, *eg* washing, shaving, having a bath, putting our make-up on, or household tasks, *eg* cooking, cleaning, ironing, DIY, tending the garden.
3. 'You' time	This is the time we devote to other people – socialising with friends, visiting relatives.
4. 'Our' time	This is the time we devote to our intimate relationships.
5. 'My' time	This is the time we set aside to pursue our own interests and hobbies.
6. Alone time	This is the time we spend in our 'head', imagining, fantasising, meditating.
7. Battery charging time	This is the time we spend relaxing, sleeping.

CLOCKING IN TO YOUR ATTITUDE TOWARDS TIME

There are three particular enemies of time:

1. Perfectionism.

2. Workaholism.

   (We saw a lot of these two attitudes in the 'A' type Alan Case Study 4 in Chapter 2. Read the case study again to see if you can identify with any of Alan's attitudes.)

3. Procrastination.

Perfectionist?
Spend time re-doing tasks?
Give yourself and others a hard time?
Need approval all the time?
Set yourself high/impossible standards most of the time?

Workaholic?
Neglect 'me' time?
Avoid 'you' time?
Work round the clock?
Work even when it's holiday time? Weekends? Bedtime?
No play time?
Get irritated when people interrupt your work time?
Get more excited about your work than any other time?
Friends, family have given up expecting you on time?
Think about your work when relaxing? Driving? Falling asleep?
Others are speaking?
Talk about your work most of the time?
Working long hours has hurt your family? Damaged your
relationships?

Procrastinator?
Prefer to have a whale of a time?
Drag your feet in the mean time?
Wind others up by wasting time?
Put off 'til tomorrow things you don't what to do in today's
time?
Afraid of failure, so won't take a risk and commit your time?

Do you say to yourself:
I might do it later.
I'll do it another time.
I wish it would go away.
It's too risky!
I can't face doing that today?

Procrastination is the thief of time.

Edward Young

Fig. 17. Defining your attitude to time.

Side-tracked Simon (Case Study 18 in this chapter) is an example of someone who errs on the side of procrastination. Spend a few minutes of your time reading this case study to see if Simon's attitudes ring any alarm bells for you. Also read through the statements in Figure 17 to see whether they have a familiar ring about them. If they do, you could well benefit from doing a time and motion study of what gets in your way of using your time to your best advantage.

ACTIVITY 25 – Calculating how you structure your time

Time is like a river made up of the events which happen, and its current is strong; no sooner does anything appear than it is swept away, and another comes in its place, and will be swept away too.

(Marcus Aurelius)

To calculate the amount of time you spend on each of the seven different ways of structuring time, write the corresponding number in each of the segments on the chart in Figure 18. For example, if between 7 am and 8 am you are getting ready for work or having breakfast, this would be number 2. If you spend an hour talking with your partner between 7 am and 8 am, this would be number 4. In your personal development journal keep a record for one week of how you structure your time.

ACTIVITY 26 – Analysing how you have spent your week

From your journal records you should now have a clearer picture of how you spend your time each day. The next stage is to analyse how many hours you have spent this week on each of the seven areas:

Serving time
Domicile time
'You' time
'Our' time
'My' time
Alone time
Battery charging time

To enable you to get a complete picture of how you have spent your week, prepare yourself a piechart, dividing it into seven segments: the size of each segment corresponds to the amount of time you have spent on each area. Figure 19 gives an example:

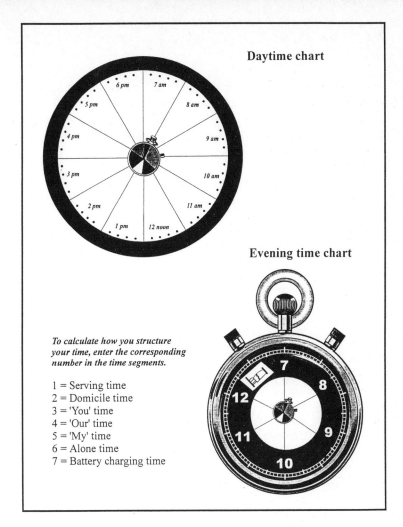

Daytime chart

6 pm · 7 am
5 pm · · 8 am
4 pm · 9 am
3 pm · 10 am
2 pm · 11 am
1 pm · 12 noon

Evening time chart

To calculate how you structure your time, enter the corresponding number in the time segments.

1 = Serving time
2 = Domicile time
3 = 'You' time
4 = 'Our' time
5 = 'My' time
6 = Alone time
7 = Battery charging time

Fig. 18. Calculating how you structure your time.

Battery charging time
Domicile time
Serving time
'Our' time
Alone time
'Me' time
'You' time

Fig. 19. Weekly time chart.

EXAMINING YOUR WEEKLY TIME CHART

Look closely at your chart. How does it look?

- Are some segments much bigger than others?

- Are there any segments missing? If there are, how do you feel about this?

- Which of the seven ways of structuring time have you found most satisfying? Which have you found least satisfying?

- Would you like your segments to look different? How would you like them to look now? In six months' time?

The fact is we cannot make time, so to change how your chart looks means making adjustments to the way you spend your time. What adjustments could you make that would allow you more time to do the things you find satisfying?

EXPLORING THE IMPORTANCE OF PLAY TIME

> Dost thou love life? Then do not squander time, for that's the stuff that life is made of.
>
> (Benjamin Franklin)

To enjoy life, we all need to have some pleasure, fun and laughter (play time). However, time pressures in adult life can get in the way of play time, or we may feel guilty playing – as if it's something adults shouldn't do! Yet today, leisure centres are springing up all over the country – and what are they after all but adult play centres!

Identifying your play time gets lost
Early childhood
Children learn to develop through play. Play is encouraged. It's acceptable to play. Children go to *playschool*, have fun with their *playmates*.

School years
There is an emphasis on studying and learning. Play gets relegated to second place. Specific times are allocated to *play time*. Specific places are designated for play, *the playground, playing fields*.

Late teens/early twenties
There is an emphasis on studying and achieving, resulting in little *play time*. Any spare time may be taken up seeking a *sexual playmate*.

Adulthood
It's mating time. Our time is committed to others – building a nest, rearing the fledglings, pursuing a career, all of which is time consuming, hence *play time* goes out of the window.

ACTIVITY 27 – Rediscovering the child in you
Allow yourself plenty of time to complete this activity.

Read through the following list of childhood pastimes and games. Do any of them trigger memories for you?

- playing marbles or dabstones
- playing hide and seek
- making sandcastles
- making/flying a kite, making model aeroplanes
- tiddler fishing
- collecting stamps/bus tickets
- skipping
- hopscotch
- acrobatics
- pitch and putt
- swimming, football, cricket, rugby, hockey
- amateur dramatics
- playing a musical instrument
- writing, reading, drawing, painting
- dancing, singing
- doing jigsaws.

Close your eyes and turn the clock back
Imagine you are five. Reflect on who you used to play with and what you did to have fun.

- What did you most enjoy doing at the age of five?
- What games did you like playing?

Now imagine you are ten. Reflect on who you used to play with and what gave you the most pleasure.

- What did you most enjoy doing at the age of ten?

- What games did you like playing?

Open your eyes
Think about whether you are still doing any of those activities you enjoyed as a child (some people turn their childhood hobbies into a career).

Moving the clock forward
Are there any of those childhood pursuits that would give you pleasure today? Consider:

- How could you adjust your time to fit in some fun activities?

- Where could you go to play them?

- Who would you like to play them with?

- Would you need a refresher course to rediscover your creativity (for example, a painting class, badminton lessons)?

- Were there any fun activities you dreamed about doing as a child, but never had the opportunity? Could you take up any of these missed opportunities now?

ACTIVITY 28 – Prioritising your time at work
Do you:

1. Start your day with a clearly written plan of what you have to do?   Yes/No

2. Prioritise what you need to attend to urgently?   Yes/No

3. Prepare your plan in the form of a daily timetable, breaking your day into 30/60 minute slots, showing what you plan to do in each?   Yes/No

4. Allow sufficient time in your plan for unforeseen problems or distractions?   Yes/No

5. Build 'thinking time' into your plan?   Yes/No

6. Keep an appointment diary of forthcoming meetings and events?   Yes/No

7. Allow for the fact that you may perform better
   at certain times of the day?   Yes/No

8. Take into account that certain tasks (especially
   creative ones) utilise a lot of time and mental
   energy, and allow time for a change?   Yes/No

9. Review what you have achieved at the end of the
   day, and rewrite a plan for the following day?   Yes/No

10. Give yourself a 'pat on the back' for a job
    well done?   Yes/No

GETTING MORE ORGANISED

Figure 20 gives some tips for getting more organised. However,
beware of becoming obsessive about keeping lists – don't let them
rule your time. They are useful in that they can help you organise
your time and tasks efficiently, and can save you valuable time
looking for pieces of paper or expending mental energy trying to
remember what it was that was so important.

Dealing with procrastination

> Even if you're on the right track, you'll get run over if you just
> sit there.
>
> (Will Rogers)

Ever say to others: 'I wish you'd stop dilly-dallying around and
make a decision', or 'I can't understand why you don't get on and
finish that job', or words to that effect? If you have, the chances are
you are dealing with a procrastinator. Perhaps you err on the side of
procrastination yourself? Either way, procrastination can be
frustrating.

People procrastinate – for example, act evasively, stall for time,
make excuses, delay, postpone, put off or aside, or shelves things –
for a variety of reasons. Often procrastinators fear failure or
criticism, feel victimised or overwhelmed, or get side-tracked when a
better offer comes along. Whatever the reason, pinpointing the root
cause can lead to a solution as it did for Simon.

CASE STUDY 18 – SIDE-TRACKED SIMON

Simon came for stress counselling, because his wife was threatening

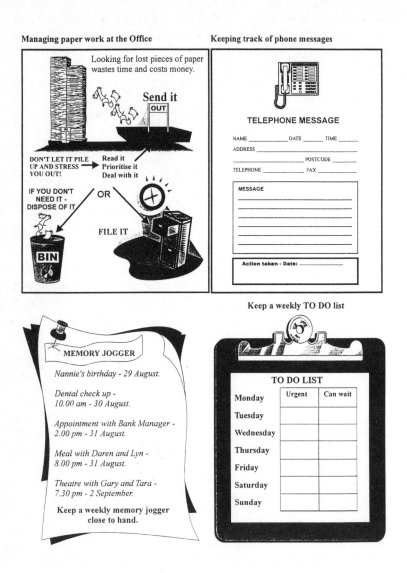

Fig. 20. Tips for getting more organised.

to leave him. Not because she didn't love him, but because he was forever making promises to do jobs around the house, which he failed to keep. With the best will in the world, he would start the promised tasks, but never managed to complete them. Simon was a good starter but a poor finisher. He got easily side-tracked, and found managing his time efficiently very difficult. When we looked at how he planned his day, we discovered that *not planning his day* was one of the major problems.

Wasting valuable time
Each morning, he would sit contemplating which job to tackle first. He had so many on the go, the thought of completing even one had become formidable. Some of the jobs he'd started were beyond his capabilities, but rather than ask for help, or employ someone to finish them, he sat hoping they would go away.

Prioritising tasks
Our work together involved looking at all his outstanding tasks, and prioritising them. He delegated the ones he couldn't manage, and formulated a plan for tackling the others, in small manageable steps. This motivated him into action, and within a couple of weeks he completed a major job he had started three years previously.

Planning ahead
Feeling good about what he'd achieved, he then moved on to finish his other long outstanding tasks, which increased his self-confidence, and put him back in his wife's good books. Through counselling, Simon learnt how to manage his time constructively, how to ask for help, and that leaving things unfinished leads to stress.

ACTIVITY 29 – Overcoming procrastination
Use your personal development journal for this activity.

1. Write down all the tasks you have been putting off, and consider the reasons why you are putting them off.
2. Try to identify what you are saying to yourself about these tasks (your mind-talk menaces). Write these down.
3. Note which task you have been putting off the longest. Is it the most difficult? Do you need help to complete it? Would you feel a great sense of relief if this task was completed? Yes? Then it's time to take action.

Make an action plan

Make this your priority task, and think about what you need to do to complete it. Can you break the task down into more manageable chunks? If it is too difficult, can you delegate it to someone else, or get someone to help you?

Compile a list of the steps you need to take to get this task completed

Now stop procrastinating, get on and take that first step. Who knows, you might find it wasn't half as difficult as you anticipated!

Repeat this exercise with all the tasks on your list you have been putting off, bearing in mind that the longer you leave things, the more of a problem they might become, and the harder they can be to sort out.

Note: Sometimes it's important to delay taking action, especially when you have an important decision to make that could affect your life or other peoples', and where you need 'thinking it over time'. This is different from procrastination. In this case the following quote is worth keeping in mind:

> Wisely and slow; they stumble that run fast.
>
> (*Romeo and Juliet*, William Shakespeare)

KEEPING YOUR PERSONAL DEVELOPMENT JOURNAL

> The value of life lies, not in the length of days, but in the use we make of them; a man may live long, yet live very little. Satisfaction in life depends not on the number of your years, but on your will.
>
> (Michel de Montaigne)

In your journal prepare a time profile as presented here.

• I manage my time well in the following areas:

_____

_____

• I waste time by:

_____

_____

- I could manage my time better if I:

  _____

- I would like to spend more time on:

  _____

  _____

- I would like to spend less time on:

  _____

  _____

- I can adjust time for the things I enjoy doing by:

  _____

  _____

9

Setting and Accomplishing Your Goals

The secret of success is constancy to purpose.

(Benjamin Disraeli)

The final, yet very important step in learning to thrive on stress is to master the art of setting and accomplishing your goals. Goals give us a sense of direction and purpose – something to aim for. Achieving goals can provide a great sense of achievement and reward, as well as raising self-confidence and self-esteem.

SETTING GOALS

Imagine you are driving from Liverpool to London for the first time, and you haven't allowed yourself time to plan your route, or you thought you could find your way without a road map. The chances are you will get lost en route, or your journey might take you twice as long as anticipated. You might even decide it's too difficult and return home. By setting a clear goal of where you want to go, and mapping out your route carefully, you increase your chances of arriving at your final destination successfully, reduce the risk of getting lost on the way, and are less likely to give up if the going gets a bit difficult. Figure 21 shows the six Ds of effective goal-setting.

FOLLOWING THE SIX Ds OF EFFECTIVE GOAL-SETTING

It helps to view the six Ds of effective goal-setting as a set of carefully formed objectives (the stepping stones that will keep you on target to achieving your aim). Each step is important, and following them in the order presented will increase your chances of successfully accomplishing your goals.

> Like archers, we will stand a far great chance of hitting the target if we can see it.
>
> (Aristotle)
>
>
>
> **DEFINING**
> ↓
> **DIVIDING**
> ↓
> **DECIDING**
> ↓
> **DESIGNING**
> ↓
> **DOING**
> ↓
> **DIAGNOSING**

Fig. 21. The six Ds of effective goal setting.

Example: Writing this book

1. Goal: My goals were to write a book about stress management and get it published.

2. Objectives: The stepping stones that enabled me to accomplish my goal were:

- Belief in myself – that I had the confidence and skills necessary to write the book.

- Ensuring I had the necessary tools, *ie* computer, software, printer.

- Preparing a book outline and title.

- Finding a suitable publisher.

- Planning the book contents.

- Setting myself a realistic time-scale for writing the book, taking into account other work commitments, running a home, time for family and visiting friends, leisure activities.

- Determination to see the project through to completion.

Without setting these objectives to keep me on track, my goals might never have been achieved, and you would not be reading this book!

Being specific

It's important to be specific when setting goals. For example, a goal of wanting to get on better with your boss or partner is generalised and vague. A goal of wanting to *communicate better* with your boss or partner is a more clearly defined goal. It's also vital to be realistic, as goals set too high may produce stress, while goals set too low might result in procrastination. When setting a goal it helps to ask yourself the following questions:

- 'How important is it to me to achieve this goal?'

- 'How will I feel if I achieve this goal?'

- 'Is my goal realistic and achievable?'

- 'Have I got the confidence and skills necessary to achieve my goal?'

- 'Have I got the time and the determination to succeed?'

OBSERVING THE 6 Ds IN ACTION

To demonstrate the goal-setting process in action, let us follow two people working through the steps.

CASE STUDY 19 – PLUCKY PAULINE

Step 1: Defining a goal

Pauline had been divorced for eight years. Since getting divorced she had been too busy to think about forming another relationship. She'd had sole responsibility for bringing up her daughter and running the home, and she worked full-time. When her daughter left home to get married, Pauline began to feel a bit lonely and isolated. Although she enjoyed her own company most of the time, she felt ready to form a new relationship, but was unsure of the best way to go about meeting a potential partner. She decided to follow the six Ds of effective goal-setting. **Pauline's defined goal (step 1) was to meet a potential partner**.

Step 2: Dividing a goal

Pauline brainstormed all the ideas she could think of that could help her meet a potential partner (see Figure 22).

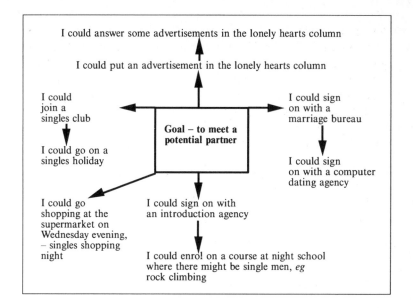

I could answer some advertisements in the lonely hearts column

I could put an advertisement in the lonely hearts column

I could join a singles club

I could sign on with a marriage bureau

Goal – to meet a potential partner

I could go on a singles holiday

I could sign on with a computer dating agency

I could go shopping at the supermarket on Wednesday evening, – singles shopping night

I could sign on with an introduction agency

I could enrol on a course at night school where there might be single men, *eg* rock climbing

Fig. 22. Dividing the goal – Pauline's brainstorm of ideas.

Step 3: Deciding

It was time for Pauline to make her mind up about which idea appealed to her most. She favoured the idea of placing an advertisement in the lonely hearts column. Her second choice was to sign on with a computer dating agency. It's useful to keep a reserve option up your sleeve in case your first idea doesn't work out as planned. Pauline then went on to weigh up the pros and cons of pursuing her idea.

Pros

- I don't have to reply to anyone I consider unsuitable.

- Seeing how many replies I get will be interesting.

- It will get me out of the house in the evenings.

- It will be good to have some male company again.

- It shouldn't cost me too much to place an advertisement.

Cons

- I might be putting myself at risk.

- I will feel embarrassed meeting a total stranger, and won't know what to say.

- If I do meet someone it might mean giving up my independence.

Pauline's next task was to look at how she could strengthen her pros (the positives), and how she would weaken her cons (the negatives).

Strengthening the pros and weakening the cons
This is the list Pauline prepared.

- I am outgoing and friendly, and I'm not normally lost for words.

- Other people have told me they enjoy my company.

- I relate well with the men I work with.

- I find other people fascinating, and am a good listener.

- Replies will be addressed to a box number, so there's no risk of anyone discovering where I live.

- I can phone anyone who sounds interesting to see if I feel the same after I've spoken to them. It would be advisable to do this from a payphone for two reasons:

  1. They won't be able to trace my home phone number.

  2. If I don't like the sound of the person, I can pretend my money has run out.

- I have my own transport so if I decided to meet anyone, I could arrange to meet them on neutral territory, and choose a place where I know there will be plenty of other people around.

- It will give my self-confidence a much needed boost.

- It will get me out of a 'comfortable' rut.

- It could be fun meeting new people, and if I do meet someone suitable it doesn't necessarily mean I'll have to give up my independence. I could make it clear that it's important for me to have time to myself, and time for visiting my friends and pursuing my hobbies.

- If I don't take the risk I could be on my own for ever.

Step 4: Designing a plan
Here are the objectives Pauline set herself (the stepping stones to achieving her goal).

1. I will devote Monday evening to reading the adverts in the lonely hearts column of the local newspaper. I'll also ring the newspaper to enquire about the cost.

2. I will spend Tuesday evening drafting some adverts. I will try to be as creative as possible – perhaps I could write it in the form of a 'ditty' or poem so it will stand out! This might increase the number of replies.

3. On Wednesday I will ask my friend Sarah which one she thinks is the best.

4. I will fax the advert to the newspaper on Thursday, so it will go in next Monday's edition.

Step 5: Doing

Pauline put her plan into action. She drafted several adverts. This is the one her friend Sarah liked the most:

> *Professional carer*
> *has vacancy for male carer.*
> *The post is voluntary but in return*
> *I can offer warmth and mutual support.*
> *I am a unique second-hand model (produced 1955),*
> *and due to regular maintenance*
> *look good, and am built to last.*
> *I am a sleek attractive mini*
> *with smart exterior and soft interior.*
> *I've suffered a few knocks and covered some miles,*
> *but my batteries have been recharged*
> *and I now prefer life in the slow lane.*
> *I have a tendency to smoke a bit*
> *and am not adverse to a little lubrication.*
> *I enjoy parking at*
> *restaurants, theatres, leisure centres,*
> *by the beach or in the countryside.*

Pauline's advertisement was an overwhelming success – she received a large bundle of letters, and had great fun reading them all. The reply that appealed to her most was from a like-minded poet. Here is part of it:

> *If life begins at 40*
> *Then I've just reached my teens*
> *I'm gregarious and friendly,*
> *yet soft behind the scenes.*
> *It's said I'm built like Tarzan*
> *but alas there is no Jane,*
> *Are you the one to light my fire*
> *so 'I beat chest' again?*

> *I enclose the telephone number of my tree house*
> *– please give me a bell.*

Step 6: Diagnosing

The final step was for Pauline to diagnose whether she had been successful in accomplishing her goal. The answer was yes. She arranged to meet 'Tarzan' and they very quickly became inseparable soul-mates. They married two years later.

CASE STUDY 20 – PUFFING PATSY

> To cease smoking is the easiest thing I ever did. I ought to know because I've done it a thousand times.
>
> (Mark Twain)

Step 1: Patsy's defined goal was to give up smoking

Step 2: Dividing a goal

Patsy brainstormed all the ideas she could think of that could help her achieve her goal (see Figure 23).

Step 3: Deciding

It was time for Patsy to make her mind up about which idea appealed to her most. She felt she could benefit by using many of the ideas she had come up with. She then went on to weigh up the pros and cons of giving up smoking.

Pros	*Cons*
● My health will improve.	● I might put on weight.
● I will be financially better off by about £1,000 a year.	● I might find it difficult to relax.
● The house will smell fresher.	● I won't know what to do with my hands.
● I won't smell like a dirty ashtray.	● I might not be able to cope without a cigarette.
● My boss will be delighted.	● It's been a big part of my life for 36 years.
● I won't have to stand outside in the freezing cold at work.	● I'll lose one of my pleasures in life.

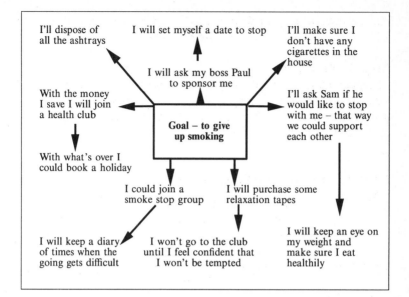

Fig. 23. Patsy's brainstorm of ideas.

- It will improve my breathing.
- It will improve my circulation.
- My eyes won't get so sore.
- My mouth will taste fresher.
- I won't have to wash my clothes and hair every day.
- I'll be nicer to be near.
- I will decrease the risk of getting lung cancer.
- I will lose my smoker's cough.
- I will not get so many colds.

Having identified the many advantages of giving up smoking, Patsy decided she didn't need to strengthen her pros or weaken her cons. She therefore moved on to step 4.

Step 4: Designing a plan

Here are the objectives Patsy set herself (the stepping stones to achieving her goal).

1. Date set to stop.   Sunday 8 September
    Sunday is a good day because I am not under a lot of pressure on Sundays.

2. 8 September (morning)   Dispose of all ashtrays, and ensure I have no cigarettes left in the house.

3. Tell Sam that I am stopping smoking on Sunday 8 September and ask him if he will stop with me. If he's not ready to stop, ask him if be will be as supportive as possible by not leaving his cigarettes lying around.

4. Ask Paul if he will sponsor me to stop smoking.

5. Before Sunday 8 September buy myself some relaxation tapes.

6. Call in at the surgery and enquire about the dates of the smoke stop groups. Ask if I can join the next group.

7. Saturday 7 September. Spend leisurely morning at the Travel Agents. Book a weekend away at the end of September as an incentive to keep going. Also call in at the Leisure Centre and enquire about membership fees.

8. On Sunday 8 September. Plan a change of routine. Have a lie in until 9.00 am. Spend 30 minutes relaxing in a hot bath. Eat a healthy breakfast and then go to Kew Gardens. Have lunch in a restaurant. Request a non-smoking area. In the evening play a game of chess with Sam. Give myself a pat on the back for making it through the first day.

9. Dealing with setbacks. If the craving gets too much and I succumb to having a cigarette, don't give myself a hard time. Accept that smoking is an addiction and it's hard to give up an addiction. It won't help me if I beat myself up over it. Acknowledge that I've had a slip, not a major relapse, tell myself that I'm not a failure and get back on track.

10. Prepare myself a list of warning signs about the dangers of smoking and stick them up in strategic places around the house.

11. Design a daily wall planner and tick off every successful day.

12. Constantly remind myself of how well I am doing.

We'll leave Patsy preparing to take her action, as by now you will hopefully have grasped the idea and feel ready to have a go at working through the 6 Ds yourself.

ACTIVITY 30 – Goal-setting

Step 1: Defining a goal
Record in your journal a goal you would like to achieve within the next three months. Make it a fairly simple goal to begin with until you become more familiar with the process. Remember, your goal needs to be specific, realistic and achievable.

Step 2: Dividing the goal
Brainstorm all the ideas you can think of that could help you achieve your goal.

Step 3: Deciding
It's make your mind up time. Select the idea that appeals to you most. Next identify the pros (the things that can help you achieve your goal), and the cons (the things that are against you achieving your goal. These may be internal factors such as anxiety or fear, or they may be external such as lack of money, time, support.

Strengthening your pros and weakening your cons
Review your pros and cons list, and then consider any ideas you can think of to strengthen the pros and weaken the cons.

Step 4: Designing a plan
Objectives: Set yourself a series of objectives (stepping stones) to reach your goal. Rank your objectives in degree of difficulty – 1 being the least difficult and 5 being the most difficult. You may decide you need more or less than 5 depending on the goal you have set yourself. Add further objectives if necessary.

Time scale: Set yourself a date for achieving each objective. Be realistic, otherwise you might put yourself under unnecessary pressure.

Step 5: Doing

It's time to put your plan into action. Keep your plan close at hand to keep you on track. Each time you achieve one of your objectives give yourself a reward, and remind yourself how well you are doing.

Step 6: Diagnosing

The final step is to diagnose whether your action has proved successful. Ask yourself the following questions:

1. Have I achieved my goal?
2. Have I partly achieved my goal?

If your idea did not work out according to plan, ask yourself:

1. Was the goal I set myself realistic?
2. Was the time scale I set myself for achieving my objectives realistic?
3. Was the idea I chose the best one?
4. Do I need to adapt my plan or repeat some of the steps?
5. Would it help to go back to my list of ideas and try another?

Whatever you decide to do, the important thing is you have been successful in having a go. You have:

- Defined a goal.
- Divided your goal into more manageable chunks.
- Decided on an idea for achieving your goal.
- Designed your plan of action.
- Done the taks you set yourself.
- Diagnosed the results of your action.

It is common sense to take a method and try it. If it fails, admit it frankly and try another. But above all, try something.

(Franklin D. Roosevelt)

KEEPING YOUR PERSONAL DEVELOPMENT JOURNAL

The reward of a thing well done is to have done it.

(Ralph Waldo Emerson)

1. Record the difference between a goal and an objective.

2. Record one long-term, realistic goal, that you would like to achieve.

   Lay down, or sit in a comfortable chair, and close your eyes. Practise abdominal breathing, and as you breathe out repeat the word RELAX to yourself. When you feel totally relaxed:

   - Imagine in your mind's eye how you would feel achieving this goal.

   - Imagine yourself in your mind's eye achieving this goal.

   - Imagine in your mind's eye what life would be like if you achieved this goal.

   - Plan in your mind's eye the steps you need to take to achieve this goal.

   - When you are ready, slowly count to ten and bring yourself back to the room.

   - While the steps are fresh in your mind, record them in your journal, and set yourself a date to start putting your plans into action.

   Never lose sight of your goal. Keep it in your mind's eye and focus on it regularly. **The mind is a very powerful tool – used wisely it can help you achieve your goals**.

3. Record the key learning points for you in this chapter.

4. Record the key learning points for you in this book.

5. Record how your life has changed as a result of learning and practising the techniques in this book.

6. Record what you plan to do next to build on this learning.

   Note: I wish you well on your journey in the future. It has been a privilege to share my learning with you, and I hope it has helped increase your learning.

   God, give us the grace to accept with serenity the things that cannot be changed, courage to change the things that should be changed, and the wisdom to distinguish the one from the other.

   (Reinhold Niebuhr)

Glossary

Abdominal breathing. Breathing from the lower part of the chest – reduces tension, anxiety and panic.

Adrenalin. Hormone released by the body when person feels 'threatened'. Prepares the body to fight or take flight.

Affirmations. Brief self-statements, affirming the positive. For example, instead of 'I am useless' – 'I am a worthwhile person'.

Alternative therapies. Acupressure, acupuncture, Alexander Technique, aromatherapy, Bach Flower Healing, massage, hypnotherapy, Reiki Healing, reflexology.

Anger. Generated by the fight response. Prepares the body for action.

Anxiety. Tension in the mind, the body, the whole self.

Assertiveness. Clear and honest communication.

'A' type personality. Extremely competitive, achievement oriented, impatient, hard-driving, aggressive (which may be repressed). At risk of stress.

Autogenic training. Series of mental exercises which reduce stress and aid relaxation.

Biofeedback. Involves the use of electronic instruments to measure stress levels. Used in conjunction with physical and mental relaxation exercises.

Brainstorming. Generating a free flow of thoughts.

Breakdown. Can result from excessive overload of stress and may lead to deep depression or heart attacks.

Burnout. Chronic fatigue.

Conditioning. The beliefs, attitudes, feelings and behaviours we learn from our parents or other significant authority figures.

Empathy. The ability to see things from another person's point of view – to put yourself in their shoes. Being non-judgemental.

Exercise. Useful for reducing the risk of heart disease, helps with weight control and has positive psychological effects.

Fear. Generated by the flight response. Prepares the body to flee from the threat.

Fight or flight response. If a situation is perceived as threatening, the body prepares us to take action – face the threat (fight) or run away from the threat (take flight).

Four components of stress. Mental, physical, emotional and behavioural symptoms.

Hardy personality. Easy going, adept at maintaining a healthy balance between work and play. Tends to cope well with pressure.

Hyperventilation. Overbreathing (rapid and shallow). Panic attacks are triggered by hyperventilation.

Negative mind-talk. Our private thoughts – silent voice. Tends to lead to negative feelings and self-defeating behaviour.

Non-verbal communication. Body language. Includes eye contact, body posture, mannerisms, gestures, tone of voice.

Optimum stress. Peak performance stress – a healthy level.

Panic attacks. Magnified and irrational form of fear. Sufferer becomes overwhelmed by anxiety.

Useful Contacts

The following useful contacts are provided for information purposes and do not necessarily constitute a recommendation.

Accuracy *about* Abuse, PO Box 3125, London NW3 5QB. Tel: (020) 7431 5339. Fax: (020) 7433 3101.Email: moor@aaastar.demon.co.uk. Website: www.accuracyaboutabuse.org

Age Concern, Astral House, 1268 London Road, London SW16 4ER. Tel: (020) 8765 7200. Fax: (020) 8765 7211. Email: ace@ace.org.uk. Website: www.ace.org.uk

Al-Anon Family Groups UK & Eire, 61 Great Dover Street, London SE1 4YE. Offers understanding and support for families and friends of problem drinkers, whether the alcoholic is still drinking or not. Alateen, a part of Al-Anon, is for young people aged 12–20 who have been affected by someone else's drinking, usually that of a parent. Tel: (020) 7403 0888 (24 hour helpline service). Fax: (020) 7378 9910. Email: alanonuk@aol.com. Website: www.hexnet.co/uk/alanon/

Alcoholics Anonymous, PO Box 1, Stonebow House, Stonebow, York YO1 7NJ. Tel: (01904) 644026. Fax: (01904) 629091. Website: www.alcoholics-anonymous.org.uk

Alcohol Concern, Waterbridge House, 32–36 Loman Street, London SE1 0EE. Tel: (020) 7928 7377 (Mon to Fri, 9.00 am – 5.00 pm). Fax: (020) 7928 4644. Email: alccon@popmail.dircon.co.uk
Website: www.alcoholconcern.org.uk

British Association for Counselling, 1 Regent Place, Rugby, Warwickshire CV21 2PJ. Tel: (01788) 550899. Information Line: (01788) 578328. Fax: (01788) 562189. Email: bac@bac.co.uk. Website: www.counselling.co.uk

British Association of Psychotherapists, 37 Mapesbury Road, London NW2 4HJ. Tel: (020) 8452 9823. Fax: (020) 8452 5182. Website: www.bap-psychotherapy.org

Bristol Crisis Service for Women, PO Box 654, Bristol BS99 1XH. Particular focus on self-injury. Provides training and consultancy. National helpline: (0117) 925 1119. Contact times: Friday and Saturday evenings 9.00 pm – 12.30 am. Website: www.users/zetnet.co.uk/BCSW/

Carol Spiers Associates (International occupational stress consultancy), Gordon House, 83–85 Gordon Avenue, Stanmore, Middlesex HA7 3QR.

Tel: (020) 8954 1593. Fax: (020) 8907 9290. Email: CSA@stress.org.uk. Website: www.stress.org.uk/csa

Centre for Stress Management, 156 Westcombe Hill, London SE3 7DH. Tel: (020) 8293 4114. Fax: (020) 8293 1441.
Website: www.managingstress.com

ChildLine UK (Free national helpline for children and young people in trouble or danger). Tel: 0800 1111 (freephone)
Website: www.childline.org.uk

Eating Disorders Association (for help and understanding around anorexia and bulimia), First Floor, Wensum House, 103 Prince of Wales Road, Norwich, Norfolk NR1 1DW. Helpline: (01603) 621 414 (9.00 am – 6.30 pm, Monday to Friday). Youth Helpline: (01603) 765 050 (18 yrs and under 4.00 pm – 6.00 pm Monday to Friday). Admin only: (01603) 619090 (9.00 am – 5.00 pm, Monday to Friday).
Email: eda@netcom.co.uk Website: www.gurney.co.uk/eda

International Stress Management Association(UK), Division of Psychology, South Bank University, 103 Borough Road, London SE1 0AA. Tel: 07000 780430. Fax: (01992) 426673. Website: www.isma.org.uk

Mind*info*Line, Granta House, 15–19 Broadway, London E15 4BQ. Tel: (020) 8522 1728 (London), 0345 660 163 (outside London). Open: Monday to Friday 9.15 am – 4.45 pm. Provides a mental health information service to anyone who contacts them by letter or telephone. Website: www.mind.org.uk

No Panic, 93 Brands Farm Way, Telford, Shropshire TF3 2JQ. Voluntary charity. Aims to help people who suffer from panic attacks, phobias, obsessive compulsive disorders and other relaxed anxiety disorders. Helpline: (01952) 590545. Information line only: Freephone 0800 783 1531. Office: (01952) 590005. Fax: (01952) 270962.

NSPCC (National Society for the Prevention of Cruelty to Children). Tel: 0800 800 500 (free helpline). Website: www.nspcc.org.uk

Relate, Herbert Gray College, Little Church Street, Rugby CV21 3AP. Tel: (01788) 573241. Fax: (01788) 535007. Website: www.relate.org.uk

Stresswise, PO Box 5, Congleton, Cheshire CW12 1XE. Mail order for biodots and relaxation tapes, *Teach Yourself Managing Stress* (book). Tel/fax: (01260) 274294. For details of stress management and stress awareness courses for industry and the professions. Tel: (0161) 247 1234. Fax: (0161) 247 6325. Email: T.Looker@mmu.ac.uk

The Institute of Counselling, 6 Dixon Street, Glasgow G1 4AX. Offers distance learning courses in counselling and stress management. Tel: (0141) 204 2230. Fax: (0141) 221 2841.
Website: www.collegeofcounselling.com

The Institute of Family Therapy, 24–32 Stephenson Way, London NW1 2HX. Offers counselling and therapy to couples and families, and individuals wanting help with relationship issues. Tel: (020) 7391 9150. Fax: (020) 7391 9169. Email: ift@psyc.bbk.ac.uk

The Samaritans, 10 The Grove, Slough, Berkshire SL1 1QP. Over 200 branches in the UK and Ireland. Provides confidential and emotional support to any person who is suicidal or despairing (24 hour a day service – all year round). Tel: (01753) 216500. Fax: (01753) 775787. Website: www.samaritans.org.uk. *Note*: For your nearest branch consult your local telephone directory.

Westminster Pastoral Foundation Counselling & Psychotherapy, 23 Kensington Square, London W8 5HN. Tel: (020) 7937 6956. Fax: (020) 7937 1767. Email: counselling@wpf.org.uk *or* training@wpf.org.uk Website: www.wpf.org.uk

Workaholics Anonymous, PO Box 11466, London SW1V 2ZQ.

USEFUL WEBSITE

www.stress.org.uk (links to specialist associations, organisations and other useful information). British based. A good place to begin browsing.

LOCAL INFORMATION

The best sources for local information are:

1. GP practices who will put you in touch with local services available.
2. *Yellow Pages* – look under section Counselling and Advice.
3. CAB (Citizens' Advice Bureau). Branches in most large towns. Look in *Yellow Pages* under Social service and welfare organisations.
4. Councils of Community Service.
5. Local newspapers often provide a list of helpline telephone numbers.
6. For details of training courses contact your nearest adult education department, college or university.

Further Reading
and Other Useful Resources

Alcohol
Alcohol: Minimising the Harm: What Works? Martin Plant, Eric Single and
Tim Stockwell (Free Association Books, 1997).
Women and Alcohol: Contemporary and Historical Perspectives, Moira Plant
(Free Association Books, 1997).

Anger management
Calm Down, Dr Paul Hauck (Sheldon Press, 1974).
Managing Anger, Gael Lindenfield (Thorsons, 1993).
The Dance of Anger, Harriet Goldhor Lerner (Pandora Press, 1989).

Assertiveness and self-confidence
Assert Yourself, Gael Lindenfield (Thorsons, 1986).
Assertiveness at Work: A Practical Guide to Handling Awkward Situations
(2nd edition), Ken Back and Kate Back with Terry Bates (McGraw-Hill,
1991).
Assertiveness: The Right To Be You (Claire Walmsley (BBC Books, 1991).
A Woman in Your Own Right, Anne Dickson (Quartet Books, 1982).
Be Assertive, Beverley Hare (Optima, 1990).
Dare to Connect: How To Create Confidence, Trust and Loving Relationships,
Susan Jeffers (Piatkus, 1992).
How to Cope with Difficult People, Alan Houel with Christian Godefroy
(Sheldon Press, 1994).
Managing Conflict, Ursula Markham (Thorsons, 1996).
Super Confidence, Gael Lindenfield (Thorsons, 1989).
The Positive Woman, Gael Lindenfield (Thorsons, 1992).

Body language and communication
Body Language: How to Read Others' Thoughts by Their Gestures, Allan
Pease (Sheldon Press, 1984).
Body Language in Relationships, David Cohen (Sheldon Press, 1992).
Don't Say Yes When You Want To Say No, Herbert Fensterheim and Jean

Baer (Futura, 1987).
What Do You Say After You Say Hello? Eric Berne (Corgi, 1990).

Counselling and therapy

A Complete Guide to Therapy: From Psychoanalysis to Behaviour Modification, J. Kovel (Penguin, 1991).
How To Counsel People at Work: A Practical Approach to Staff Care, John Humphries (How To Books, 1995).
Learning to Counsel: How to Develop The Skills to Work Effectively With Others, Jan Sutton and William Stewart (How To Books, 1997).
On Being a Client: Understanding the Process of Counselling and Psychotherapy, David Howe (Sage Publications, 1993).
Self-Counselling: How to Develop The Skills to Positively Manage Your Life, William Stewart (How To Books, 1998).
The Counselling Handbook: A Complete Guide to What to Expect and How to Get the Counselling You Need, S. Quilliam and I. Grove-Stephenson (Thorsons, 1990).
Who can I talk to? The User's Guide to Therapy and Counselling, J. Cooper and J. Lewis (Hodder & Stoughton, 1995).

Depression
Depression and How to Survive it, Spike Milligan and Anthony Clare (Ebury Press, 1993).
Depression: The Way out of Your Prison, Dorothy Rowe (Routledge, 1983).
Down With Gloom! or How to Defeat Depression, Professor Brice Pitt and Mel Calman (Gaskell, 1993).
Post Natal Depression: Your Questions Answered, Erica Harvey (Element Books, 1999).
Understanding Depression and Finding Freedom, Dorothy Rowe (Thorsons Audio, 1999).

Families/parents/relationships
Families and How to Survive them, Robin Skynner and John Cleese (Mandarin, 1990).
How to Cope with Difficult Parents, Dr Windy Dryden and Jack Gordon (Sheldon Press, 1995).
Life and How to Survive it, Robin Skynner and John Cleese (Mandarin, 1994).
Men are from Mars, Women are from Venus: A Practical Guide for Improving Communications and Getting What You Want in Your Relationships, John Gray (Thorsons, 1993).
Rebuilding: When Your Relationship Ends, Dr Bruce Fisher (Impact, 1993).
Sex and Relationships, Rosemary Stones (Sheldon Press, 1998).
The RELATE Guide to Better Relationships, Sarah Litvinoff (Vermilion,

1992).

The Ties that Bind: A Survival Guide to In-Law Relationships, Sylvia Bigelsen (Element Books, 1999).

Toxic Parents: Overcoming Their Hurtful Legacy and Reclaiming Your Life, Dr Susan Forward with Craig Buck (Bantam Books, 1989).

Health and alternative therapies

Alexander Technique: An Introductory Guide to Natural Poise for Health and Well-being, Richard Brennan (Element Books, 1999).

Aromatherapy: A Practical Approach to the Use of Essential Oils for Health and Well-being, Julia Lawless (Element Books, 1999).

Beat Fatigue with Yoga: A Step-by-Step Guide, Fiona Agombar (Element Books, 1999).

Complete Book of Men's Health, Dr Sarah Brewer (Thorsons, 1999).

Complete Foot Reflexology, Kevin and Barbara Kunz (Thorsons, 1999).

Flower Remedies: An Introductory Guide to Natural Healing with Flower Essences, Christine Wildwood (Element Books, 1999).

Homeopathy: An Illustrated Encyclopedia of Safe and Effective Remedies, Dr Christopher Hammond (Element Books, 1999).

Massage: A Step-by-Step Approach to the Healing Art of Touch, Stewart Mitchell (Element Books, 1999).

Meditation: An Introductory Guide to Relaxation for Mind and Body, David Fontana (Element Books, 1999).

Natural Heart Health: How Women Can Prevent or Reverse Heart Disease, Linda Ojeda (Thorsons, 1999).

Practical Aromatherapy (4th edition), Shirley Price (Thorsons, 1999).

Reflexology: Therapeutic Foot Massage for Health and Well-being, Inge Dougans (Element Books, 1999).

Reflexology for Women, Nichola Hall (Thorsons, 1999).

Shiatsu: The Complete Guide, Chris Jarmey and Gabriel Mojay (Thorsons, 1999).

Think Slim: If You Think You Can't be Slim, Think Again, Eve Brock (Vermilion, 1992).

Think Yourself Slim: A Unique Approach to Weight Loss, Carol Harris (Element Books, 1999).

Insomnia

Insomnia: Your Questions Answered, Dr Dilys Davies (Element Books, 1999).

Jealousy

Jealousy and Envy, Dr Windy Dryden (Sheldon Press, 1999).

Jealousy: Why it happens and how to overcome it, Dr Paul Hauck (Sheldon Press, 1991).

Loss and bereavement
Gifts of Tears: A Practical Approach to Loss and Bereavement Counselling, Susan Lendrum and Gabrielle Syme (Routledge, 1992).
Grief Counselling and Grief Therapy: A Handbook for the Mental Health Practitioner (2nd edition) J. William Worden (Routledge, 1995).
On Death and Dying: Elisabeth Kubler-Ross (Routledge, 1995).

Motivation
Self-motivation: Developing Self-reliance, Persevering with Challenges, Gael Lindenfield (Thorsons, 1996).
Successful Motivation in a Week, Christine Harvey (Hodder & Stoughton, 1998).

Overcoming fear

Feel The Fear And Do It Anyway, Susan Jeffers (Arrow, 1991).
Positively Fearless, Breaking Free of the Fears that Hold You Back, Vera Peiffer (Element Books, 1999).
Overcoming Your Fears, Shirley Trickett (Sheldon Press, 1999).

Panic attacks
Don't Panic, Sue Breton (Optima, 1994).

Personal development
12 Easy Ways to Nourish the Inner You, Gael Lindenfield (Thorsons, 1999).
60 Ways to Change Your Life, Lynda Field (Element Books, 1999).
60 Ways to Heal Your Life, Lynda Field (Element Books, 1999).
A Challenge to Change: An Inspirational Workbook, Beechy and Josephine Colclough (Thorsons, 1999).
Choosing a Better Life: An Inspiring Step-by-step Guide to Building the Future You Want, Hilary Jones and Frank Gilbert (How To Books, 1999).
Emotional Excellence: A Practical Guide to Self-Discovery, Maya Phillips (Element Books, 1999).
Further Along the Road Less Travelled, M. Scott Peck (Pocket Books, 1997).
Hiding What We Feel, Faking What We Don't: Understanding the Role of your Emotions at Work, Sandi Mann (Element Books, 1999).
Know Yourself! Self-awareness Activities for Nurses and other Health Professionals, Philip Burnard (Whurr, 1997).
The Power of Letting Go: A Practical approach to Releasing the Pressures in Your Life, Patricia Carrington (Element Books, 1999).
The Road Less Travelled, M. Scott Peck (Arrow Books, 1990).
Woman Power, Lynda Fields (Element Books, 1999).

Positive thinking

A Positive Thought For Every Day, Dr Windy Dryden (Sheldon Press, 1998).

More Positive Thinking: How to Create a Better Future for Yourself, Vera Peiffer (Element Books, 1999).

Positive Thinking: Everything You Have Always Known About Positive Thinking But Were Afraid to Put Into Practice, Vera Peiffer (Element Books, 1999).

Positive Under Pressure, Gael Lindenfield and Malcolm Vandenbugh (Thorsons, 1999).

The Power of Positive Living, Norman Vincent Peale (Cedar, 1992).

The Power of Positive Thinking, Norman Vincent Peale (Cedar, 1990).

Your Can if You Think You Can, Norman Vincent Peale (Cedar, 1982).

You Can't Afford The Luxury of a Negative Thought, John Roger and Peter McWilliams (Thorsons, 1990).

Problem solving

How to Solve Your Problems, Brenda Rogers (Sheldon Press, 1991).

Self-esteem and self-image

60 Tips for Self-esteem: Quick Ways to Boost Your Confidence, Lynda Field (Element Books, 1997).

Building Self-esteem: How to Replace Self-Doubt with Confidence and Well-being, (2nd edition) William Stewart (How To Books, 1999).

Creating Confidence: The Secrets of Self-Esteem, Rex Johnson and David Swindley (Element Books, 1999).

Low Self-Esteem: Your Questions Answered, Elaine Shechan (Element Books, 1998).

Self-Esteem, Gael Lindenfield (Thorsons, 1995).

The Beauty Myth, Naomi Wolf (Vintage, 1991).

The Highly Sensitive Person: How to Thrive When the World Overwhelms You, Elaine N. Aron (Element Books, 1989).

Your Total Image: How to Communicate Success, Phillipa Davies (Piatkus, 1990).

Self-harm and child sexual abuse

Breaking Free: Help for Survivors of Child Sexual Abuse (new edition), Carolyn Ainscough and Kay Toon (Sheldon Press, 1998).

Healing the Hurt Within: Understand and Relieve the Suffering behind Self-destructive Behaviour, Jan Sutton (How To Books, 1999).

Stress and anxiety

90 Days to Stress-Free Living: A Day By Day Health Plan including Exercises, Diet and Development of Willpower, C. Norman Shealy (Element Books, 1999).

Controlling Anxiety: How To Master Fears and Phobias and Start Living With Confidence, William Stewart (How To Books, 1998).

I'm Too Busy to Be Stressed: How to Recognise and Relieve the Symptoms of Stress, Dr Hilary Jones (Hodder & Stoughton, 1997).

'Managing' Stress: Emotion and Power at Work, Tim Newton with Jocelyn Handy and Stephen Fineman (Sage Publications, 1995).

Managing Workplace Stress, Susan Cartwright and Gary L. Cooper (Sage Publications, 1997).

One-Minute Stress Management, Dr David Lewis (Cedar, 1993).

Stress: Your Questions Answered, Rochelle Simmons (Element Books, 1997).

The Complete Guide To Stress Management, Dr Chandra Patel (Vermilion, 1996).

Time management
Better Time Management, Jacqueline Atkinson (Thorsons, 1992).

MENTAL HEALTH PROFESSIONALS' CATALOGUE

Smallwood Publishing Group, The Old Bakery, Charlton House, Dour Street, Dover, Kent CT16 1ED. Tel: orders (01304) 226900. Information (01340) 226800. Fax: (01304) 226700. Website: www.smallwood.co.uk. Email: k.smallwood@smallwood.co.uk

Smallwood Publishing Group is a mail order supplier of innovative books and other resources. Their catalogue lists details of hundreds of resources.

INTERNET ADDRESSES

Web sites where you can order books (often at discounted prices).

- www.amazon.co.uk (UK branch of Amazon: carry a huge range of books)
- www.bol.com (British bookshop)
- www.blackwell.co.uk
- www.bookshop.co.uk (owned by W. H. Smith)
- www.waterstones.co.uk
- www.barnesandnoble.com (huge US bookshop)
- www.amazon.com (huge US bookshop)

Index